M000078722

generation
nanny

Hey Nannies,
mamas, and Denver Women!
I hope you find your way, just
as I did mine, walking all around
the neighborhood of Denver. ♡ Thanks
for all you do, Keep going! xoxo-
Audrey Brazeel

Please share and pass on!
Follow me @generationnanny
#GenerationNannyDenver

AUDREY BRAZEEL

Copyright © 2020 by Audrey Brazeel

All rights reserved. No part of this publication may be reproduced, distributed or transmitted in any form or by any means, including photocopying, recording, or other electronic or mechanical methods, without the prior written permission of the publisher, except in the case of brief quotations embodied in critical reviews and certain other noncommercial uses permitted by copyright law. For permission requests, write to the publisher at the address below.

Generation Nanny
Austin, TX
GenerationNanny.com

Cover Design: Melody Christian of FinickyDesigns.com
Book Coach/Editor: Amy Collette of UnleashYourInnerAuthor.com

Ordering Information: GenerationNanny.com

Quantity sales: Special discounts are available on quantity purchases by nonprofit organizations, corporations, associations, clubs and others. For details, contact us at GenerationNanny.com

GENERATION NANNY / Audrey Brazeel —1st ed.

ISBN: 978-0-578-69215-9

Author's Note

Much of this book was written in my twenties and thus, my perspectives and opinions have changed over time. I accept my 20-year-old brain for what it was: naïve and jaded, but I try to infuse it with wisdom from my past and an informed perspective from my present. If you find yourself reflected in a character in my stories, thank you for sharing your truth with me. Some people featured in this book may be surprised by how they are portrayed or what I thought of our time together; in any case, you all helped me grow and I am thankful for our time together.

The stories from the past are fictional narratives inspired by real conversations. The historical recollection of my mother's Nanny, Teen, has been constructed from various interviews, memories, and stories my family has told me over time. Though this is a true story, the names and identifying details of the people have been changed to preserve their privacy. If you're a mom, a nanny, a millennial, or all three, I hope this narrative gives you power in knowing that your journey, though twisted and misshaped, is being orchestrated by someone greater than us. Embrace it for what it is and don't forget to give thanks to God and the Universe along the way.

Thanks

Thank you to my family, friends, and my husband for supporting my crazy dream of writing a book. I am so grateful for all of the people who helped me crowdfund in 2019, your money helped my dream of publishing become a reality. Special thanks to my grandmother, aunts, and mother for sharing their recollections of Teen with me and for their acceptance of how I chose to share them.

I am forever grateful to my mother. Her patience, her acceptance, her heart, and for always telling me that I am a great writer. I would not have had the confidence, nor the courage, to do this if not for your words, Mom!

Thank you to Amy Collette, for your steadfast mentorship and for all the time you have given me to verbally process… everything! You have been far more than a book coach, editor, and publisher—you have been a life-guide for me, helping me create something that has given me purpose and direction. Thank you!

Dedication

This book is dedicated to the women who care for our children, to those who clothe us and bathe us, and to those who keep us safe. This book is dedicated to the women of the past, and of the future, who will continue to do such selfless acts of service for others. Most of all, this book is for Teen.

Table of Contents

Preface

I spent my twenties in a perpetual job search. When the going got really tough, I did what I did best at this time in my life. I ran the other way. I turned to nannying as my income-placeholder and did my best to run from decision making, disappointment, and adulting.

Instead of reveling in my perceived youth, nannying forced me to mature. My nannying back-up plan began to transform into my lifestyle, and I spent three years nannying for seven families in a row, and traveling across the country.

I began journaling as a therapeutic assignment given to me by a counselor in 2014, and this reflective practice morphed into a series of narrative stories about human connection, recognition and privilege, perseverance and perspective, childcare and education, and the strength of women.

Nannying gave me purpose, as writing this book has given me purpose.

People spend their lives trying to find their purpose. We search for purpose through our career choices, our relationships, religion, family, art, or hobbies. Growing up in the digital age, millennials have been bombarded with examples of ultimate success, and thus they have created a romanticized idea of what it means to make an impact. Not everyone can become the CEO of a company, and not everyone can start their own NGO to solve world hunger. We have come to believe that if we are not making a notable, shareable, recognizable impact, our life somehow lacks meaning.

I want *Generation Nanny* to help redefine what it means to make an impact in today's world. As I discover the importance of simply caring for others, I try to confront and analyze my own privilege, race, culture, class, and bias. I did this the best I know how, and hope I am able to accurately represent some of my viewpoints and pay homage to nannies who have come before me. Most importantly, I hope this honors Teen's[1] ephemeral spirit and her life's work as a nanny.

Our society's priorities are all mixed up. They are backwards, upside down, and value money and power over anything else. Like many people, I struggle with finding my place in the world, but in an age where women are using their voices to ignite change, I want this book to reveal a universal truth: When women bind together to support each other's families, careers, and lives, anything is possible!

---

[1] Learn about Teen in Chapter 2: For Teen

GENERATION NANNY TIMELINE

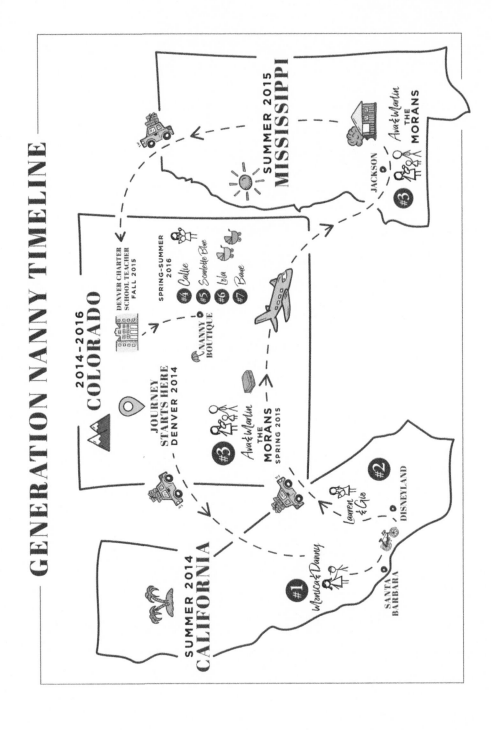

PART I

CHAPTER ONE

For Generations

I was sitting in the passenger seat of my aunt's bronze Lexus sedan, riding north along highway 84. Leaning with the twists and turns of the desert landscape, we were singing at the top of our lungs to our favorite Dixie Chicks song, *Wide Open Spaces*. Our destination was a dusty little compound in Northern New Mexico called Ghost Ranch.

The point was to spend a few days "roughing it," as my aunt was well versed in all things Ritz Carlton. For one full day and one night she agreed to share a bathroom with a stranger in a crappy cabin, and paint, hike, and do nature things with me, her hippie girl. Ghost Ranch was run by locals, while seasonal staff, basically white baby boomers, ran the maintenance and anthropological museum in exchange for free room and board—primitive feels, but without the dirt floors.

This was a long overdue reconnection for my aunt and me, as our previous encounter had been my college graduation five years before. We spent my graduation weekend arguing about Obama over hors d'oeuvres and had reluctantly agreed to disagree on just about everything. Words were exchanged. Eyes were rolled. We never talked about that weekend again.

Now, five years later, in 2017, reality television star and billionaire businessman Donald Trump had been elected president. I expected some arguments about Trump, but I was pleasantly surprised that his name never came up. I can say with confidence that if Trump gave me anything during his time in office, it was, ironically, more unity between my Republican extended family and me. At least both sides could agree on one thing: Trump was certifiably insane and most definitely tweeting more than he was presidenting.

The well-known painter Georgia O'Keefe had spent many years painting the landscapes and desert scenes that surrounded Ghost Ranch. Towering rock formations colored by layers of pink coral dirt and iron-rich clay made for a bizarre and shockingly Mars-like setting. Georgia had a home in Ghost Ranch in the early 1930s through the 1960s. With actual primitive dirt floors, she was one of the first females to pioneer and embody Horace Greeley's, "Go West Young Man" mentality. Her story is cool. Of course, I connect with it as I grew up in the Southwest, living in Colorado and often venturing down to see my family in New Mexico. I feel a dorky kinship to this artist who is long gone, but after reading the shortened version of her biography that I bought in the gift shop, I thought she was pretty freaking rad.

We were on a pilgrimage to pay homage to Georgia's legacy. My aunt and I had always bonded over arts and crafts when I would visit her in Santa Fe. She was my "cool aunt" who taught me how to make purses out of old Levis from the thrift store and let me watch PG-13 movies. I'll never forget watching *Fools Rush In*, with Salma Hayek and Matthew Perry (aka Chandler Bing). It was my first run-in with a movie about an interracial relationship; Latina cocktail waitress Isabel Fuentes Whitman and white guy Alex Whitman, beating the odds of cultural and dialectic language differences and falling in love. I also really enjoyed watching *Save the Last Dance*, for obvious reasons. Interracial relationships were my jam.

To the O.G. New Mexicans at the time (Native American and Spanish descendants from settlers of the 16-19th century), Georgia O'Keefe was just some crazy white lady who had the privilege of choosing to live primitively as an artist selling thousands, maybe millions, of dollars' worth of paintings. The same landscapes and scenes that native peoples had been painting for centuries but have yet to make a dime off of... smells like white privilege.

Settling into our desert cabin with a suitemate from Norway, we put our political opinions aside and committed to rekindling our artsy-fartsy, aunt-niece connection. It worked! Paintings were painted, sulfur water was showered in, we may have seen a ghost that my aunt refused to acknowledge but police brutality and the rise of white supremacy was only mentioned once, so, I call that a win!

On our way back to Santa Fe from Ghost Ranch, I took advantage of the time I had alone with her in the car. Quizzing my aunt, I asked her to recall some of her memories of her nanny, Teen.

Teen essentially raised her, her three sisters, and two younger brothers. This set of six kids included my mom of course, the youngest girl in the family.

My aunt was one of the middle children, third from the top, born in the late 1950s, coming into adolescence in the 1960s and 1970s. She was a middle child all right. "Miss Independent," her father called her. She wore loud and groovy handmade apparel and taught herself how to create her own small retail business of handmade terry-cloth bathrobes and hair wraps. Perfect for the Southern sorority girl, new mom, or nanny, I'd like to think. I was a model for her company back in 1993. I was even featured in a mail catalogue. This is now my only claim to fame.

She moved out of Arkansas after college, making her own way in the Aquanet capital city of Dallas, Texas. She dated a conservative number of successful men and claims to have seen the Dixie Chicks in a cafe when they first started. She lived the Southern version of *Sex and the City*, as I, a child of the 1990s and 2000s pictured it. My aunt's life is unique in comparison to her brothers and sisters. She certainly took a path that led her away from her small-town upbringing, woven with annual trips to Paris, art galleries, food, and travel. Though she found her home in New Mexico far away from the muddy Saline River in Arkansas, you could feel her commitment to her roots and hear it in her thick accent.

She shared with me the impact that Teen's death had on her during her college years. "Cristeen was her full name, but we called her Teen. Mama and Daddy finally made her go to the doctor when they noticed how sick she looked. She had never been to the doctor before in her whole 60-plus years of life! Not long after that, she passed. My biggest regret is that she didn't live long enough for us to take care of her."

The way she described her relationship with Teen showed me a side I had never seen before. Always matter-of-fact and certain, my aunt was rarely vulnerable. Seeing her in this light was refreshing and revealed how Teen was not just her Nanny, but that she had been a part of shaping her identity and impacted her whole life.

As she described to me her feelings about Teen, it became more obvious than before, the profound and lifelong impact caretakers have on the children and the families they work with. As we grow older, our childhoods affect us indirectly. Moments in our intimate relationships or friendships as adults might sometimes mirror how we're brought up. Our bodies and minds grow and develop, but our childhood is something that forms us beyond our comprehension.

Teen's impact spans across generations of children. Starting with my mother, I know firsthand how she reaped the benefits of Teen's warm touch and calm demeanor. My mother was a better parent to me because of her, and I will be a better parent to my children because of her.

I am compelled to pay tribute to Teen's work and honor all of the nannies who have nurtured past generations of children. We owe them at least this much.

When popular culture remembers the history of the nanny position in America, we picture black and brown women dressed in white and blue uniforms, holding white babies, cooking food for aristocratic families in small bible-belt towns. This history is portrayed in the book and 2011 film, *The Help,* when finally, the experiences of women of color in the early 1950s and 1960s were being shared in widespread media. The thing about a film creating our historical memories is the backlash it earns from history critics, and rightfully so. At this time, it has yet to be followed by a more historically accurate version, though I have faith it will eventually be re-created, filmed, and directed by women of color.

Roxanne Gay, feminist writer, professor, editor, and commentator, put it simply when she said, "If you go to the theater without your brain (leave it in the glove compartment), *The Help* is a good movie." She explained in her various essays that most popular films regarding African-American history and slavery have been primarily created by white people, for white people to hear history in the way they want to remember it. Well, it worked. My family loves to preface their childhood as being "like *The Help,"* referring to the happy moments they want to remember while conveniently forgetting the societal disenfranchisement maids and nannies were victim to at the time.

The narrative cannot solely be shaped and formed by this Hollywood blockbuster as it presents a romanticized rendition of what it was like to be a woman of color working in the Jim Crow South. Their recollections weren't meant to be hurtful, but they also weren't actively being helpful either. In the same sense, in order to avoid being another white woman romanticizing the black experience, I do not claim to speak for Teen as I can only speak from the perspective of the children she cared for.

Though the memories my family shares are rosy and sweet, I could never know how Teen truly felt about her life raising six white kids and none of her own and I yearn to see Teen as a whole person, a person with humanistic qualities and with hopes and desires that have nothing to do with serving anyone but herself. I know she must have had these thoughts as every woman I have ever met often thinks about the things she could do if she simply had more privilege, or if she were a man, had more money, more children, fewer children, a better upbringing, or access to more education; how her life could have been different.

While writing this book I decided that I cannot tell my story without shedding light on the experiences of women of color who have been tucking in children for nap time, bathing and feeding them, answering, "Yes, Ma'am" and "No, Ma'am," for centuries. This is an experience that I, as a white millennial nanny, can only attempt to grasp and one I can never compare to.

I am privileged enough to have the ability to follow through with executing my dreams and act on my hopes and desire for more. I had the safety net of my family's financial support, the comfort of knowing I have an education to fall back on, and so much more.

It is important to remember that women of color have been performing domestic work throughout history. Many of them were unable to act on their dreams because of institutional, cultural, and linguistic barriers created by sexism, racism, and patriarchy. These barriers are still actively blocking women of color today and it's about time we make moves to change this. Organizations who advocate for fair wages, safe working environments, and job security for those who perform domestic work are mobilizing and making a difference, and their work is changing the world for the better. Domestic workers' rights are necessary components of the women's liberation movement, and they need greater attention.

I aim for my book to be a part of the bigger conversation around domestic labor laws and to paint a picture showing the complexity of a woman's experience as a nanny in the 21st century. Being a nanny is a vulnerable, sometimes undesirable, position for any person to be in at times. On a daily basis, I would like to believe that most people who choose this role get up in the morning with a want and a desire to love, care, and to give; but considering many women in history were not given the choice to be nannies, this work should be seen as one of the most gracious and selfless acts of all time.

It takes a remarkably higher level of love and compassion to care for others in the capacity that Teen did for my mother, my aunt, and all of their siblings. I intend to share her impact and only parts of her story the best I know how, by sharing information I learned through interviews and exchanges with my family.

Teen would have been 96 years old on March 31, 2020. May her memory live on through all of us and through generations of nannies to come.

CHAPTER TWO

For Teen

Teen, the selfless, the gracious, the irreplaceable.

When I was younger, my mom would share memories spent with her nanny more often than memories with her own mother. I never found that odd, as I was completely oblivious to what it would be like to have a nanny or anyone else caring for me other than my own mom. As these stories have been sprinkled throughout my life, Teen's significance is irrefutable, and I have her to thank for so much in my own life.

"Teen had soft brown skin that always felt so good. She would rub my back until I fell asleep every night," my mother said. Her memories flood my mother's thoughts, and though I had heard some of these stories a thousand times, I always let her tell them, never rushing. I watched her blot the tears from her cheeks, cleaning up any mascara drippage that occurred while recounting the sweet moments they shared.

My mom is one of six; eight years separate the oldest to the youngest. Her house was always full and busy with people, especially during the summer. Surrounded by the dense woods of southern Arkansas, Fulton is a town of a little over 6,000 people. Known for tall pines and the local apple production, its nickname is the "Apple Capital," complimented by an annual festival every October.

"Bill Clinton himself rode in the Apple Parade right before he became president! I've got a picture!" This fun fact is rarely followed up with the memory that Bill made a frat house out of the White House.

Fulton was the place for families to live the American dream and raise their children, experiencing a boom in the 1950s that seemed to last through the late 1970s. With a church on every corner, one glorious Sonic diner, a drive-in movie theater, one "inside theater" with air conditioning, a YMCA, a country club, a police department, and one fabulous parade every summer, Fulton was in a dry county and had all the wholesome feels for folks moving away from poverty and crime-ridden cities like Little Rock and Memphis.

If you were white, you could certainly find solitude in small towns across America as you tried to escape the ongoing trend of integration where you could raise your family in a peaceful town where whites lived wherever they want and all the black and brown friends will make sure to stay on the outskirts. Don't worry, you don't have to see them if you don't want to, as they'll be forced to continue going to school with their own, church with their own, and swim with their own until 1968.

Newly and poorly integrated schools brought the children together, but in the adult world it was still us versus them. Fulton is one of the many towns in the Jim Crow South that may not be implanted in our historical memories like Selma, Alabama, but it shares many of the same stories of people believing that separate but equal was good enough.

My aunt was still recalling details about Teen to me as we made the first turn back onto highway 84. "I think Mama paid her something like $100.00 a week? Or maybe every two weeks?"

I quizzed my aunt with ferocious curiosity, trying not to sound outraged by the wage she'd just uttered. "Was that enough to get by then? How often was she there? Where did Teen live?"

My aunt couldn't recall her schedule, but she did say she doesn't remember Teen not being there. I guess overtime wasn't a thing back then.

"I think she must have taken off Sundays. I mean, she must have, but momma and daddy would often go away for a weekend. They were socialites and went to the races, New Orleans, dinners, and parties all the time," my aunt said. (I was totally picturing Great Gatsby right then.) "We had a night nanny named Esther who would stay with us, and another young high school girl would come over to help iron. Teen was always there though, for all our birthdays, everything! One time on my birthday, Momma and Daddy were on their way to a New Years' party that night. Momma let me know there was a birthday cake in the icebox for me. I'm not sure if I ate it with Teen, but I'm sure she was there for that too."

Teen pressed the bedsheets at the beginning of every week, taking them straight from the dryer to the ironing board. My mom remembers the ever-present beads of sweat on Teen's upper lip while she watched her move about the house doing her tasks.

Even my mother, a trained debutant, never understood the point of ironing children's bedsheets; "They'll surely be all wrinkly by the time someone lays on them. I don't see the point." she shared.

During rare moments as a nanny, when the children have been fed, the dishes washed, the clothes folded; you finally have a moment to come up for air. Some, if they can, take that moment to take a break, but women like Teen find something to do. I always felt that when I was "on the clock" I should come up with something to do to earn the money I was making. Does that mean I ironed their bedsheets? Hell no.

But Teen, she went over and beyond and it shines a light on what nannies were expected to do back then.

The summers were hot and muggy in Fulton, cicadas creaking loudly in the trees, the smell of people burning leaves. My mom figured Teen worked from 7 a.m. to 9 p.m. and said Sunday was her day off.

My grandparents spent many weekends going out, driving to nearby towns for dinners and up to Hot Springs for the horse races and gambling. He was one of two attorneys in the town, and she was a housewife who had spent the last eight years being perpetually pregnant.

After her sixth child in 1962, my Grandma called it quits. She said she couldn't have done it without Teen's help. "It's strange because she was 'the help,' but she was with me through all the children's births. It felt like we were friends. She was just always there." My grandmother has a Scarlet O'Hara way of speaking. "There" sounds like "they-a." She was born into a white-collar family who owned real estate and had been cared for, cooked for, and cleaned up after her whole life by her maids, cooks, and housekeepers.

"That's just the way it was back then." That's what my family says when I ask them questions about Teen and the other people who helped my family for decades. *You don't choose how you grow up. You don't choose what race you are, or where you are born. What are you to do about things you cannot change?* I ask myself.

Knowing this history of my own family plagues me with guilt for having such a privileged ancestry of people who had children and families without a worry in the world. They had the ability to hire people to help them accomplish their dreams and raise a family. They were able to pass on the simple gift of freedom, choices, safety, acceptance, and access to things. Things that white people think are endowed on us when we are brought into this world, but people like Teen never had this chance.

This guilt that I feel, that some people feel, when looking back on history and knowing your ancestors were players in a societal game of racism and oppression, is called White Guilt.[2] White guilt is useless, if not used to create positive social change. Though I found being a nanny frustrating and sometimes belittling, it was actually a privilege that I have had the opportunity to learn from and now to create positive social change with.

During the summer of 1965, my grandmother left the two youngest children with Teen for a week. My grandmother recalls pulling out of the driveway headed to Disneyland with the four older kids. My mom and the baby of the family, Bobby, almost 4 years old, stood in the kitchen sink watching the station wagon pull out of the driveway. My grandmother remembers her babies waving goodbye through the window as Teen stood behind them ready to brace their fall if they lost their footing. She specifically recalls this scene, and though she never shared her true thoughts of what it feels like to leave your babies for days at a time, her memory reflects her confidence in Teen's ability to care for them.

I wonder about this time that Teen spent with two toddlers in a big empty house for over a week. I wonder if she freely removed her shoes and played barefoot with my mother in the living room. Did she sing and laugh freely, without worrying someone would hear? She didn't have the simple pleasures I have taken for granted while being a nanny—things as natural as sharing a meal with the children, or leaving a dish or two unwashed until the next morning, playing music aloud while doing the chores for the day. I hope she did these things, and I hope she napped when the kids went down too.

Perhaps she secretly used my grandmother's perfume or looked through my grandfather's liquor cabinet out of curiosity—not that I've ever done such things.

---

[2] White guilt, or Western European guilt, is the individual or collective guilt felt by some white people for harm resulting from racist treatment of ethnic minorities such as African Americans and indigenous peoples by other white people, most specifically in the context of the Atlantic slave trade, European colonialism and the legacy of these eras. (Wikipedia, April 2020)

Back then, sharing facilities and space such as the dinner table was simply out of the question. I think about the moments I have shared with families at dinner tables and even staying the night. Certainly, I had moments where I was well aware that I was a visitor, and when they would leave, I always felt a sense of relief to do my work without someone watching or witnessing every move.

I wonder if this is how Teen felt sometimes.

Teen lived in a house near the YMCA, which at the time was a pretty nice area. It was an unexpected area for a single, African-American woman to live all alone, but I know my grandparents were pleased with their Nanny's location as it was a reflection of their well-to-do reputation.

In Fulton, even to this day, the predominantly black neighborhood is known by the locals as "Goat Neck," a nickname likely given by white people. Not much has changed in 2020, and as you drive through this area, it still has tiny shacks amidst broken down trucks, stray cats, and piles of junk in the yards.

Teen was working for one of the best families in town. My grandfather was a successful, prominent lawyer who once was compared to Atticus Finch, the attorney in the book, *To Kill a Mockingbird,* as he often could be found defending unpopular individuals. One of his favorite stories to tell us about was a man he defended who went by the name of Cornbread. My grandmother on my dad's side actually taught Cornbread in school; she even stood on the defense stand to speak on his character. I never heard the end of what happened to Cornbread, just that that was his name.

Teen had a twin sister named Darleen. The two were Cristeen and Darleen. Darleen lived in Chicago, and would for the remainder of her life. These twin sisters were living very separate lives but they would occasionally exchange a phone call or a letter with each other.

My aunt had become Darleen's pen pal when she was in grade school. "You know, I would just write, 'Hello, how are you? I am fine, school is fun, I like to draw.' Typical pen pal letters," she said. I would imagine this sweet gesture from a child cared for by her only sister was safely kept by Darleen, further connecting her to her twin from hundreds of miles away.

"Teen had no children." My mother told me: "I mean, we were her children. At one time she was married, but she never really told us what happened. I knew she had a boyfriend though. We called him Jimmy- boyfriend." This is not to be confused with Jimmy-yard man, who tended to their property. My mother recalls that Jimmy's car wasn't able to go in reverse, and she remembers watching from the window as he always took a huge circle around the edge of the property to turn around. *The nicknames, Oy vey. It's a sign of the times I guess.*

I can only begin to envision the life of Cristeen "Teen" McLean—devoting every hour of her daily life for 25 years to another family. Nannying, caretaking, cooking, cleaning, washing, and back-rubbing was her entire life. I wonder what she did on her time off. Did she read? Go to church? Dance and drink wine with friends? The difference between her age and my grandmother's was only a few years, yet, "She always called Mama Mrs. Louey," my aunt told me.

She had "unconditional love," according to my mother, who describes Teen as her confidant, feeling a very special and individualized kinship to her. "She was like my mother; she had time for me. She knew my friendships and would counsel me. We spent so much quality time talking and sharing. She helped me be accountable for my school work too."

In the sixth grade, my mom went on a diet. She wanted to try out for the cheerleading team in middle school. She ate only a single hamburger patty with ketchup for lunch all summer and dropped about 20 pounds. Maybe that's the original Atkins diet, which, with a Heinz endorsement and a healthy dose of media, had the power of producing major body image issues amongst baby boomers. "Teen completely accommodated my diet exactly the way I needed it." Developmentally, my mom was likely only beginning to perceive her own appearance in relation to others, this being a very sensitive and vulnerable stage to be in as a young girl. Another woman's support, love, encouragement, and of course guidance, cannot only help a young girl in this period in her life, but it also can help her shape her perception of herself for the rest of her life. Though my mother never shared whether Teen encouraged self-confidence or fed her positive affirmations, I would imagine she did. An 11-year-old girl never forgets her first diet, especially if it's hamburger meat and ketchup.

That summer was also in the midst of my grandmother's battle with cancer. "When I was 8 years old, my mom got cancer, and Teen was there for us a lot," my mom said. My grandmother would later reach remission when my mom entered high school, but for most of my mother's pre-teen years, Teen was there every day.

"She never seemed to go home," both my mom and aunt confirmed to me. I spoke with my mother and grandmother separately a number of times while putting this book together and, with each time, their memories grew more and more detailed.

"She gave me lots of hugs and physical affection because I did not have a lot of that from my own family," my mom shared. "She was so loyal and devoted to us. It was like she completely took us on as her own flesh and blood. She was there for every phase in my life."

"Everyone had help, but no one had help like we did, because we had Teen—very nurturing and formal in every way. She would purposefully peel an apple and serve it to a child," my mom said.

"I never saw her eat," my mom said, "I'd offer her some food and she'd say: "Nah, that's alright. I'll just smell it." She always kept her boundaries.

The confinement that both race and power have in binding maids and nannies from fulfilling their basic human needs at work leaves me feeling ashamed. Even though I trust that my grandparents treated Teen with respect and dignity, I cannot confidently say that she wasn't treated any different from any other maid or nanny during the civil rights era. I am ashamed of America, ashamed of our history of slavery. Regardless of my family's perception of their relationship with Teen, my mother, a child, was her boss, and the same racial ties that had house slaves and domestic servants bound in obedience were still in a knot at that time.

Every Christmas, Teen would come over on Christmas morning and open presents that the kids prepared for her. They watched every expression on her face as she opened each one, watching for her beautiful smile.

Did she like these gifts? Did she re-gift any of them to her sister in Chicago? So many questions I have may forever go unanswered but I liked knowing she wasn't alone.

Teen didn't drive, so my grandmother would pick her up and my mother would drive her home in their 1970s wood-paneled station wagon. She would do this for Teen all throughout high school. Teen would tap on my mother's gas gauge every time and say, "Go git cherself some gas," even when it wasn't close to empty. When my mom ran out of gas in the middle of an intersection one day, she regretted ignoring Teen's sound advice. After all the kids went away for college, Teen still came to work to cook and clean and keep my grandmother company. It wasn't too long until she fell ill.

"She helped me sell my clothing in college in a garage sale and sent me the money afterwards," my mom said, her voice high pitched and beaming. "Isn't that the nicest thing you've ever heard?"

Okay, Teen wins the best nanny award. I would never actually help in a garage sale without at least taking a little off the top for myself or coming back with an old lamp or something.

"Once we stayed the night with her. We all brought our little suitcases, and momma and daddy were thrilled that we were going to get out of the house. I was probably 4 or 5 years old, and my sisters were just a little bit older."

Again, the best nanny award goes to…

Teen grew up in a country house on a country road with her aunt. She never spoke about her mom and dad. She learned to drive a log truck, but never had a car and never went to the doctor. My grandmother's recollection of Teen's life consisted of very few details about her past or her upbringing. She didn't share much with anyone, as Teen was a true professional and the situational power that she lacked only encouraged silence.

Teen died in 1980 of a 60-pound tumor in her stomach. My mom was in college at the time and my grandfather was the one who finally forced Teen to go to the doctor.

"The student doctas had neva witnessed anything like it!" my grandmother recalled. They took Teen to Little Rock, to the University of Arkansas Medical School, where they treated African American patients for free.

After she died, my mother's family went out to the country where Teen's aunt, Ms. Warner lived, for her funeral. As the only white people in the church, my mother remembers women hooting, hollering, and crying out in pain as they grieved her death. She remembers being unable to process what had happened. Teen was clearly a beloved member of her world. Darleen, Teen's twin, came to the funeral, meeting my mother and all her siblings for the first time. "She looked just like her. It was so weird to see her at that time because Teen had just passed away. It was like seeing a ghost," my aunt said to me as we started unloading the car. We had finally arrived back in Santa Fe, the loss of Teen lingering like the dust kicked up on the dirt roads behind us.

Teen died in December, and in the spring my mom went out to the country to visit Teen's aunt.

"I drove all the way out there and knocked on the door. Her husband answered, and she was just sitting there in a rocking chair. When she saw it was me, she went back to her room and brought me Teen's wedding ring. She gave it to me as a gift, and I still have it today. It's beautiful, and has a bunch of little tiny diamonds. Must have been expensive at the time."

A few years ago, my mom gifted me Teen's ring. My mother doesn't remember Teen having a husband but she had to have been married or at least engaged before she started working for my family. There is so much we do not know about Teen's life outside of her role as a nanny, and to have an item like this allows her spirit to extend into our physical world. The trip to Ghost Ranch took place two years after my last nannying gig, and I had just begun writing this memoir. It stands as a significant time, for the stories my aunt shared with me this day helped me uncover answers to my burning questions about life and made me proud to carry on Teen's legacy as a nanny.

We owe everything to our family nanny, Teen. Her impact reaches beyond her time on earth. My family may certainly have a romanticized idea of who Teen was and her feelings towards her job, but honoring her work through the publishing of this memoir is one of the greatest honors I could ask for.

To help other nannies know and understand the value that they bring through the work they do, and the love they are disseminating over generations of people, is what I have been called to share.

With all of my heart, and all of my soul, I wish we may all continue to nurture one another and live out the legacy of love that so many women, amidst tragedy and disenfranchised circumstance, have carved out before us.

Keep on nannying on.

CHAPTER THREE

Just A Nanny

It is the summer of 2014. Katy Perry's *California Gurls* was blaring on the radio in my 2005 Ford Focus. I've called her Black Beauty, like the horse, for the past 10 years, but I just upgraded her to Black Betty, like the ACDC song. Why? Because she's a freaking badass now. This is no longer a sad, depressing story of a domesticated horse. She's earning her street cred by driving across the country to a new, though ironically more domesticated life in the sunshine state.

It wasn't but three months prior I had been dealt a few crappy cards. By crappy, I mean I had lost, and still hadn't earned, things that once were assumed to be awarded at this stage of my life. I was 25 with two college degrees and living with my parents. Also, I was single. You probably figured that out already.

I have two degrees, which is two more than Suzy Lou from high school who still lived in my hometown with two kids at this point, but what I have are social science degrees from a liberal arts college, which basically equals jack shit in job-land, so Suzy Lou might be sitting a bit prettier than me right now. With a balance of $34.61 in my savings account, driving the car I'd driven since I was 15, I was not at the point in my life that I had expected I would be.

My job with the public school district had me gridlocked from advancement. I was only making $10.15 an hour. I had been through a trillion interviews and none of them had panned out. My morale was low and waves of irrational thoughts and impulsivity were influencing my decisions.

An aura of parental disappointment followed me around like a Peter-Pan shadow, still connected at my feet. I had been dragging this feeling around with me, and I had had enough!

The rational decision would have been to stick it out and wait for as long as it has to take to get my feet on the ground. That's what most people my age did. A lot of us twenty-somethings were living at home. Why couldn't I just be patient?

Adventure is so fun, though! So I bounced around the last few years, chasing cheap rent and jobs that paid me just enough to get by, living in a transitional home for young adults, exchanging house-mom duties for cheap rent in Boulder, Colorado. I even chose to stay with a friend's mom over my own. I was willing to do whatever it was going to take to prove I could make it in the big, bad world of rising Denver property values and stagnant wages.

I wasn't the only one trying to prove to my parents that I could make it post-grad. Tons of millennials were without work, or making close to minimum wage, struggling to make ends meet while paying off their debt and trying to figure out how to use their bachelor's degree in the real world.

Where are the scissors? I'm breaking free of this Peter-Pan shadow.

My parents didn't send their daughter to college so I could become a nanny. None of my anthropology degree required changing diapers, folding laundry, or how to navigate awkward conversations with dads, but if I want to move out of my parents' house before I turn 30, I have to get creative.

I had heard of girls traveling the world, living with rich families for free and taking care of their babies. Like Angelina Jolie's nanny, "How the hell do I score a gig like that?" Unfortunately for me, "NannyforaMillionaire.com" didn't exist, so I was stuck playing my luck on Craigslist and Care.com. On my lunch breaks from my dead-end job with the school district, I picked a destination and made it my mission to get myself, at the very minimum, a summer nannying gig.

Location: I typed in: San-ta Bar-bar-a, Cali-fornia

In the Position box, I selected "Full Time, summer" from the dropdown menu of predefined positions.

The first inquiry I received was from a mother looking for a live-in nanny: "So how would you feel about sharing a room with our 8-year-old twin girls?"

"Ha! I'm 24 years old. No way." I immediately moved on to the next one.

Another family tried to convince me that working all the time doesn't mean full time work.

"Well, we really only need someone to drive our kids to and from camp. We don't need someone full-time, but just available all the time to help us in case the kids need to be picked up from camp or one of them is sick one day."

"So you want free labor?" I asked. "Nah, I'm good."

The third time was a charm. "I just need someone to cook, clean, and take my 6-year-old son to camp."

"That's it?" I was confused, but tired of scanning the internet for a way out. "Alright, I'm in."

In three days' time, I made my decision. And in seven days, I would be in the car. Though it was not the most ideal situation, I had found a family that fit my criteria just enough to pack up Black Betty and head to the beach for my summer nannying adventure.

Have you ever thought of what "throw caution to the wind" really means? According to Wikipedia, the extremely reliable and reputable source for absolute truths, it means "to do something despite the risk."

So, throwing caution to the wind, I didn't care what the recruiters would ask me when they saw the three-month gap on my resume. I didn't care that I would likely come back just as poor and unqualified as I was currently.

I needed a break—some space between me and that ever-lurking parental disappointment that was following me around waiting for me to fail again. I wanted a space to find myself, to explore the world, to live my life, even if just for the summer.

I was on my way to sunny Santa Barbara to live with a family from China as their live-in domestic servant—I mean, nanny—because that is obviously what any 25-year-old, college-educated woman would do.

I may not be nannying for Brad Pitt and Angelina in Africa or Paris, but a Chinese family in California is close enough.

I pulled out of my parent's driveway, and I couldn't help but giggle with excitement. As I merged onto the highway, I thought to myself, is this really happening?

A rush of the unknown was ahead of me and I could hardly take how happy I felt to leave the mundane behind.

After a while, I changed the dial on the radio. I tuned in to the local rock station before I started to lose service and with a slight head bang and all too real air guitar solo, *Black Betty* by AC/DC solidified my rebellious mood as I headed West towards the golden coast.

Unbeknownst to me, Santa Barbara is one of the most expensive cities to live in the United States. Due to its immense beauty and insanely high housing market, they know they can get away with whatever they want because of the staggering number of international students, hybrid surfer bums/software engineers, celebrities with vacation homes, and Oprah.

I went the cheapest route I could find. Living rent-free in exchange for cooking, cleaning, laundry, and child care. Making a measly $9.00 an hour, which is below the minimum wage in most states, I was going to make less than I made at my first job in high school wiping greasy tables at Boston Market.

"Sure! Sign me up!" That's most certainly the sound I make when desperation meets opportunity. I'd be paid to do a bunch of stuff I'd be doing anyway, besides the kid part, but I figured anything would be better than living at home.

The exchange seemed fair enough. I made the most of my weekends, spending my weekly checks in their entirety traveling around California, eating and drinking like a queen—living like I was on vacation.

Santa Barbara brought me a newfound excitement for life, for taking risks, for exploring my heart and expanding my mind. It also was freaking gorgeous and so were all the people and places I saw.

This experience is something many have told me is "interesting." Interesting is the word people use when they don't know what to say. Interesting is the word people use when they don't want to offend you and they are politely trying to cover their judgements. Former teacher turned domestic worker doesn't bring to mind dollar signs or even an intriguing career-chasing story. It's more like a backwards version of Cinderella.

Most people I attended college with at the University of Colorado-Boulder were East Coast and West Coast trustafarians—a trust fund kid disguised by Rastafarian values and a chosen bohemian lifestyle. They were working for technology start-ups in gentrified neighborhoods and going to Wing Wednesdays in Capitol Hill in Denver, scrolling through Tinder, going to Bali for yoga retreats and coming back enlightened and certifiably ready to market themselves on Instagram.

I'd like to blame a few historic events that would explain my direction, like the recession or my liberal education pushing me so far away from working for "the man" that I actually wasn't qualified to do so.

Rather, my problem was that I wanted to be in a sector that didn't necessarily want me. I was teaching for the nonprofit sector, which wasn't exactly pursuing me to fill these jobs. By "me," I mean white, monolingual, blonde, middle-upper class. My parents paid for my college out of pocket and still pay my cell phone bill and car insurance. Thank God for Obama care. While plenty of "me" were applying for these jobs, what social mission-based organizations need more of are people of color, men, and multilingual individuals who can communicate, connect, impact, and simply resemble the people they are trying to help. The last thing they need is another white woman representing diversity. I get it.

I wanted to be in the nonprofit world, though, working for the betterment of humanity. This is a genuine and honest intention, as most people have, but I was taught the importance of understanding the entire story, the power dynamics and acknowledging how white privilege plays a part in furthering historical and systematic oppression.

As much as I hate the classic narrative of the white blonde angel helping the poor brown children, that's exactly the stereotypical role I fall into. A little bit of Audrey Hepburn mixed with Princess Diana and a dash of Angelina Jolie, again with Angelina, I sense a theme. The white savior complex is real and the world was pushing back—not against me personally, though I definitely was starting to feel that way, asking, "Why was this happening to me? Why can't I get hired?" I even toyed with the concept of reverse racism, even though we all know it's not real.

I had to remind myself that this was not personal at all, that my struggle in the 21st century was a miniscule moment in history in comparison to centuries of struggles that women have battled before me.

Before I left for Santa Barbara, I had to tell my mom about the move. I was standing in the kitchen, leaning against the island towards my mother like I was making an infomercial pitch for my world-renowned product that will surely rip everyone off.

"Being a nanny is just what I need right now. I need to get out of here. I need a break from always looking for jobs that I never seem to get! When I come back, I'll be ready to get to back to work. It'll just be the summer, and how hard could it be? I mean come on. I am just nannying." This is typical of me to give long-winded disclaimers before letting others interject. My mother continued unloading the dishwasher while I spoke.

"How hard could it be?!" My mother echoed my tone, annoyed at my naive assumption that being a nanny would be a breeze. "I wish Teen were here to answer that question," she said matter of factly, while she finished putting away the rest of the silverware.

I remember being 7 years old and having one of those realization moments in school. You know, when you realize America's history isn't as full of freedom as they tell us it is? After being briefed about the meaning of Martin Luther King Jr. day, which came along with a short, 10-minute discussion about the history of the Jim Crow South, my 7-year-old brain was blown. Much of these stories had happened in the Deep South. My family was from Arkansas. I put two and two together and was disgusted, thinking, "Was this MY history?"

Before ever seeing a picture, my mom spoke about Teen so often I always assumed she was a family member. I later learned that she wasn't, she was just her nanny—just a nanny. Is there such thing?

Listening to how Teen made my mom feel, how Teen rubbed her back until she fell asleep for nearly 25 years, helped raised her five other siblings and nursed my grandmother through years of cancer treatment, she was not just a nanny.

I was starting to contextualize my parents' childhoods. When seeing pictures of my mom with Teen, I noticed her darker complexion and knew she was African American, or something, but what I became more infatuated with was her uniform. "Why was she always wearing a uniform?" You would think after a while it wouldn't be so necessary. I hated the idea of uniforms, especially in second grade when the great uniform debate had just begun across America. Wearing uniforms cut out distraction and increased learning by 12 percent, but in my first argumentative essay I wrote in fourth grade, my thesis was that of the typical 1990s child: "I don't care. I want to wear my Adidas hoodie. Let me be me."

"You'll be an amazing nanny," Mom said. She was trying to support my irrational decision-making process. "Though you seem a little overqualified," she trailed off, trying not to start an argument.

I had also had a nanny when I was an infant, and it seemed as though I was approaching a moment I never knew would present itself. I was excited that I would become a nanny myself. I almost felt like it was in my blood, like I am meant to care for others, just as Teen did for my mom and my nanny did for me.

Transported, I attempted to analyze what this means, the role-reversal and the oxymoronic nature of someone in my shoes, the shoes shined with white privilege and a college degree, stepping into a role that holds centuries of history in domestic servanthood and slavery.

I sat with this idea for a moment, struggling with the idea that nannying would be a side step away, or perhaps a step in the opposite direction of where my professional career was going. I didn't want to admit it, but nannying felt like a job that was beneath me. I knew I could do better, but in that moment, I just didn't want to do better anymore. I was tired of trying to get that nonexistent job, and just wanted to pick the easiest route and coast for a bit.

At the time, I didn't see the role of a nanny as having any more significance than being a glorified babysitter. I was wrong. It wasn't until I saw the glories and the struggles of motherhood and family life that I realized none of the women before me were just nannies. They were listeners, caregivers, sisters, confidants, nurturers, and so much more. The success of their families could be contributed to their hard work, making meals, giving rides, helping amidst divorce, illness, or separation when one or both of the parents couldn't be there. Without them, the family as we know it would cease to exist, with kids uncared for or professional careers cut short.

Women of color did not have the choice for a long time. Caring for another woman's family was once the only job they were allowed to do. Passed down from generation to generation, we have always had a high demand for nannies, which we still have today.

Many areas of the Southwest depend on immigrant women from Latin America, and in the South, young African-American women in small towns drop out of high school to fill their mothers' or grandmothers' nannying responsibilities. All the while, young white women around the country are making the conscious decision to nanny because it happens to be a great way to pay off student loans, make some heavy cash, and skip out on that thing that happens on April 15 every year.

For all of time, those who perform domestic work have primarily been disenfranchised women. Whether they are immigrants, migrants, orphaned, enslaved, indentured servants, or simply poor, domestic work has been reserved for those less fortunate to serve those more fortunate. In an effort to survive, white women, though they are still at a disadvantage because of gender, have created their own niche of domestic work by using fancy words like maid, au pair, governess, caretaker, or nanny. The titles alone help to elevate the role's status, making it more desirable to both the employer and the employee. In 21st century American, native English-speaking homes, it has become more desirable to hire an English-speaking maid, nanny, or caretaker. This desire therefore causes employers to filter out applicants who are non-

English speakers, and whatever else they don't want, whether they be fat, ugly, or brown, from the pool of applicants. They can do this without repercussion, and nothing can stop them.

I have little data to support this displacement theory, as much of this work goes completely unreported, but I know for a fact I received many of my nanny jobs because I am white, English speaking, and highly educated. The average wage for a nanny is about $15.00 per hour, which is $3.00 to $5.00 more than working at an elementary school in some states and way more than minimum wage. If you'd like to keep your Netflix account on auto-pay, nannying is a good way to go.

For the next three years, I held other people's babies, washed their sheets, and ran their dishwashers. I was happy knowing this wasn't my fate forever and that no one was forcing me to do this. I figured I was signing up for a pretty easy gig.

I was wrong. Nannying and caregiving is taxing on your body, your mind, and your soul. Being in other people's families, in their personal living spaces, and helping them run their lives leaves little to no room to run your own. Carrying the weight of the mother's to-do list while knowing her hardships as a working parent enlightened me to understand the many roles women play to continue populating the world.

Much of the success of families today should be attributed to those who too often go unnoticed—to the hidden women who have changed diapers, fixed meals, and rocked our children to sleep for thousands of years. Without them, it wouldn't be possible for women to chase their professional dreams today. It is because of them that men and women can become leaders of countries, CEOs, and Shonda Rhimes!

You know the Kennedys slept soundly all because they had multiple maids and nannies who tended to their screaming infants, helped with sleep training and entertained the children during press conferences. What are their stories?

The following stories connect my personal experience in the 21st century with those of the past and those of the future. I aim to create a deeper understanding and appreciation of the choices women must make when raising children and the caregiver's importance in women's liberation and economic prosperity.

While nannying is work of another kind, a historically insignificant position dating back to the beginning of time, I am reminded of the privilege it was to have been a part of these mother's lives. My mother and her five siblings were cared for every day of their lives by a woman who wasn't their mother. My grandfather was cared for by two different stepmothers and a long list of women who, against all odds, did what women do best—love.

CHAPTER FOUR

Santa Barbara

Between 2011 and 2014, I hadn't filed more than $18,000 per year on my taxes, and that was only for the year I had six W2s.

In 2013, I really hit the pavement applying to jobs, meaning that I stared at my computer for over eight hours a day, determined to find one that would enable me to pay my cell phone bill, car insurance, rent, and still allow me to spend more than $100.00 on food and alcohol every Saturday night. While my roommate and I sat around watching *Breaking Bad* and copying and pasting our resumes into job application websites, we were sending our well-written cover letters into cyberspace, usually to receive radio silence.

Creating more usernames and passwords to add to our growing Apple Notes for jobs like program director and administrative assistant, our hopes had run low and we quickly turned to a new solution: school.

More degrees = jobs, and more degrees = more debt. This is the vicious cycle. We educate ourselves to receive jobs to pay for the cost of educating ourselves. #21stcenturyproblems. Obama did wipe out a few people's student debt. Not that we'd be in the running for that kind of treatment when the Republicans came back into office in 2017, but a girl can dream, right?

Here goes the next feat, more usernames and passwords, testing fees, application fees, deadlines, student loan information, ordering official transcripts for $25.00 a pop, and lengthening our cover letters to cover more bases.

We would become masters of social work, public administration, organizational development and leadership, and eventually we'd pay off our student loans, and then die.

But wait, first we have to be accepted. That would be the first ingredient in this recipe, and it ended up being the hardest one to obtain.

Apparently, we weren't the only ones using this recipe.

My Dad was pissed. He wrote a letter to CU's chancellor wondering why they let me study anthropology if "they ain't got no jobs for me?" The chancellor replied, stating, "Students choose to study social science, and the demand is high, so we let them."

My Dad is still pissed, but what's new?

After reading what seemed to be the hundredth automated email signed, "best of luck in your job search," then receiving a rejection letter from the graduate school of my choice along with a break-up in the mix of course, I decided against my better judgment and hit the road. Well, Black Betty hit the road.

I was off to escape from the hard life of living at home rent free, doing free laundry, driving a car I didn't pay for and will never have to, and getting gas with the Shell card my parents so nicely paid off every month.

Really, I wasn't running away from anything. I had the privilege to get up and go, to act like this is my getaway vehicle and move to the most expensive place in the country.

I was under the impression I was at my wits' end, and I couldn't find a "real" job, I couldn't even get into school so that I could get my "real" job. My boyfriend and I broke up, and I couldn't live under the same roof as my pissed-off Dad.

Get me the hell out of here.

Rolling into town, naturally with bumper-to-bumper traffic all along the 101 in Santa Barbara, I had about two weeks to prepare for this situation and hardly gave any of it a second thought. By situation, I mean a two-room apartment with one American woman, one Chinese woman, and Danny, one 6-year-old Chinese boy.

Please hear me right. I don't mean Asian-American. I mean Chinese. Chopsticks only, shrimp balls, bao buns from Costco, and a 6-year-old who only spoke whatever dialect of Mandarin they speak in Hangzhou.

This was going to be an interesting summer for everyone.

I found myself in Santa Barbara, California, living in someone else's house.

I went to cook dinner and the only utensils were chopsticks…

What the fuck am I doing?

Traditionally, in Chinese upper-class culture, the family has a live-in nanny. This character is usually an older grandmother figure who worked manual labor throughout her life and eventually was able to advance to becoming a house slave—I mean a nanny. There is no telling what these nannies get paid in China, if at all, especially if I'm only making a lousy $9.00 an hour. Cooking, cleaning, and care-taking is the name of the game, and it is the norm for the nanny to co-sleep with the child. Chinese nannies also typically live with the family (because they must not have their own?). This is confusing my small American brain.

Sadly, this is a step up in life for many of the older women in China who wish to leave the physical labor of their jobs in factories or fields behind. It is sad to know they are no longer with their loved ones or living in the comfort of their own homes, but that's my take on the situation, my American, middle-class, white girl opinion on a cultural topic I can only try to understand. All I know is my grandma better not be taking care of anyone else's babies but mine! That is, if I ever have a boyfriend again.

I immediately tackled the co-sleeping: not gonna happen.

Cooking? Sure. I had never cooked anything more than the occasional stir fry, which was not going to fly with these people's real Asian taste buds. Upon the request of my employer, I was prompted to spend the summer cooking "real American food." Which left me wondering: what does that even mean?

Every time I thought of "real American food," I thought of things like spaghetti, pizza, and rice pilaf. I contemplated if those were American foods at all; technically, aren't pizzas and most pastas Italian? Rice pilaf is probably American—it comes in a box, and anything in a box was decidedly American food in my book. Thus, I served them Eggos and little smokies sausages for the first few weeks.

Cleaning? Sure. A few loads of laundry and a couple Clorox wipe-downs. A two-bedroom apartment can't be that hard to keep up.

As the summer passed, I learned that I am a horrible cleaning crew, and that laundry isn't exactly my forte. Let's just say I preferred throwing the laundry in, taking a bike ride, and often forgetting to dry it. "Idiot! I am the most spoiled, worst domestic servant ever."

The cooking was always a trip due to the fact that American food and Chinese food are definitely on different wavelengths. In China, they don't have a defined way of separating breakfast, lunch, and dinner foods—all are generally vegetables and starch, which is pretty deliciously basic.

Eventually the mother, Monica, said, "Well, we could have more vegetables in the morning."

You let me know when you can think of a vegetable that is served in the morning. Other than vegetables in an omelet, I couldn't think of any either. Eventually I was serving small bowls of peas and corn by request. "Whatever floats your boat, Monica."

Monica's name was inspired by *Friends*. Yes, the 1990s sitcom. Apparently, this is one of the only American-made shows they allow to air in China, and therefore Monica was inspired to name herself after an idol she must have identified with. Funny thing is, she had never considered the actor's real name, Courtney, which I personally I would argue is a much better name.

Once I made a joke with a *Friends* references as the punchline. The joke never received a reaction, just a half-smile and a nod. This is how most of my interactions with Monica would be that summer. Smile and nod. Polite, yet distant.

With a fork for me and some chopsticks for them, we had awkwardly quiet meals together every night of the week.

For nine weeks.

Nine.

Long.

Weeks.

Now, on to Danny.

Danny, Danny, Danny. What a sparkplug! What a stubborn little boy. Not that I am a psychologist, but if I were one, I would say Danny definitely has some attachment issues—classic mommy issues. Well dang, I would too, if I had co-slept with all my nannies and was never disciplined in my life. Monica told me once that in China, nannies see the child as their boss—completely flipping the natural, age equals superiority dynamic in which most adult-child relationships work. Especially with my history of being a teacher, it was a learning process for both of us to become a productive pair.

What made our being a team even more challenging was that we shared a birthday. If you know anything about the Ram, the Aries sign, it is hard-headedness and confidence that gets us through. Passionate, creative, highly emotional beings, we are typically impatient and impulsive. Aries have strong wills to go their own way without assistance. Add on the layer that Danny and I didn't speak one another's languages, we were two rams, butting heads every single minute.

This kid had some interests that one does not normally see in 6-year-olds, or at least the American kids I am used to being around. His slight obsession with a three-hour Army training documentary was just the beginning, and his love of hummingbirds and dislike of every sport was notable.

Danny was quite the character, often getting in arguments with me in Chinese and very broken English. He argued with the YMCA staff, with his mother, and often with other kids. He had the typical 6-year-old breakdowns about which door he wanted to enter through, or putting his shoes on when leaving the house. He preferred visiting the tool aisle at Sears over visiting the indoor trampoline place, which still leaves me dumbfounded.

The unique spirit of this kid couldn't be beat. By the end of the summer, he had gone to every YMCA camp they offered and was a more consistent participant than some of the full-time camp counselors.

Getting a bit better at his English, he loved to tell me "I don't want toooo," and "I know all about iiiitttt." These were perfect Aries statements of non-conformity and self-assured confidence. Our verbal communication was coming along, but it was our non-verbal that got us by on an everyday basis. Building castles with the recycled cardboard, riding on the handlebars of my bike while I walked along side it. With each day, Danny and I started to understand each other a bit more, and I was totally falling for him.

We would laugh at a few things, and he was beginning to hug me and high-five me when I picked him up from camp. I had never seen his mother hug him or show much affection. Since I wasn't co-sleeping with him (dodged that bullet), he slept with his mom all summer long. I would only hope that summer would benefit the future adult Danny and whoever he would date and one day marry. Nobody likes a man with attachment issues.

Our time ended with what I would like to call "A trip to Danny-land," also known as Disneyland with a 6-year-old. It was a bizarre yet magical, three-day adventure that felt as if I had definitely fallen through Alice in Wonderland's rabbit hole, unfortunately without hallucinogens.

Conveniently for no one, Monica had flown out a "colleague" from China to go to Disneyland with Danny and me. I was going to spend three days in Disneyland with a 6-year-old and a 20-year-old Chinese woman I did not know. My 24-year-old-self was not happy. This is not how I pictured the last three days of my summer nannying gig, but then again, this isn't how I pictured my life to go either.

This woman's main goal was to gain Danny's trust while in Disneyland and then take him back to China to be with his Dad permanently.

Step one was to gain trust. It took me two full months for Danny to do what I asked of him without running away screaming, "I don't want tooooooo." Nothing looks sketchier than a white woman chasing a little Asian boy through a parking lot while he screams in fear. No way was this plan going to be successful.

Step two was to take Danny on a 13-hour plane ride back to China without his mom or his nanny that he had just started trusting. What the hell are these people thinking?

Unbeknownst to Danny, this was his last few days with me, and his last few days in America with his mom, who wasn't even there. I didn't have the guts to tell him he was going back to China. I wasn't even sure if his mother had told him. Falling down this rabbit hole with Danny for three days was all I could give him, and I was determined to let him take the reigns—no fighting and no arguing, I committed to just let him be a kid, have a blast, and eat as much cotton candy as he wanted. The fact was that I couldn't

AUDREY BRAZEEL

change Danny's reality or nurture him to help him in the long term, so I might as well make this short term better for both of us. Whatever Danny wants, Danny gets.

Monica was seven months pregnant with her second child, and with the full intention to stay in Santa Barbara in her high-level consultant job, her husband would bring Danny back to China to start school the next month. This would allow Monica to focus on her maternity leave with her new baby in a couple of months.

None of this made sense to me. Why would a family agree to being separated by thousands of miles for so long? From what I knew, the dad didn't have any plans to move to America or for Monica to move back to China. Monica had pursued furthering her career, but also still thought it was a good idea to have a baby while she lived alone? My Western brain could not comprehend.

Yet, she was not alone, and she never would be. I had spent the summer with her and Danny, and before me there had been a number of Chinese nannies helping her while she had been in California. I learned about an entire network of Chinese nanny placement agencies in Los Angeles. They place young immigrant Chinese women, some only 15 years old, in homes of upper-class Chinese immigrants who could afford the help.

Monica wanted her daughter to be born in America. Having a girl in China raises a few red flags. If we think it is tough to be a woman in America, think about being a woman in China... Monica was a woman with a plan, and her plan included sacrifice that she never shared with me personally, but can only be compared to military wives who raise their children far away from their deployed husbands, or refugees making a new home in a foreign country without their support networks. Her decision was by choice, yes, but her decisions were based in love for her daughter's future, knowing that she wanted something more for her.

The "colleague" was suspiciously young, and I had reason to believe that she was potentially the dad's mistress. Not wanting to let my historical understanding of Chinese concubines and racist myths of polygamy frame my opinion, I gave her a chance. I mean, we had to share a hotel room. I had no choice.

This girl was close to my age, and her English was good. I wouldn't say we became friends, but it wasn't so bad to have another person there to witness Danny's outrageous fits and tantrums for once.

For three days we slept in a hotel room that cost almost $300 a night. While the "colleague" used her whitening cream on her face at night and Danny refused to bathe, I reveled in the magical atmosphere that Disneyland creates, even for adults. Though the temperature reached almost 100 degrees each day, we explored every inch of the theme park together. Holding hands, I let Danny eat cotton candy for lunch and go on any ride he chose. At this point, the struggle was over. He would be on a plane back to China in less than 48 hours, and I would rather him be full of empty calories than throwing a fit.

I held him on my back for more than two hours while we watched the infamous fireworks show. I let him be a kid—a rambunctious, energetic, 6-year-old boy. The "colleague" expressed dismay for my patience and willingness to work with Danny. She chickened out of days two and three at the theme park. I wished her the best on that 13-hour plane ride with Danny. *Sucker.*

This trip was the most fun we had together all summer, and now it was over. Saying goodbye was more difficult than I ever thought it could be. I felt numb and detached, knowing my short time caring for him would have no real influence on his development. I felt for Danny and could hardly stand saying goodbye.

With tears welling up in both of our eyes, he handed me a one-dollar bill. His only friend at camp had given the dollar to him, and he had been holding on to that sentiment of friendship all summer long. He would ask for it every morning and carry it in his pocket. This friend was the only one who would play with him, and the only one Danny never hit or pushed—such a sweet boy, LOL.

What a beautiful gesture, I thought. He gave me his prized possession as a token of love. The sweetness touched my heart.

I wished the colleague luck and I got back in Black Betty, lit myself a much-needed cigarette, and drove back to Santa Barbara from Dannyland. I could actually see the light from the bottom of the rabbit hole and felt as though I was emerging as a new woman, with more patience than I had ever had.

As I held on to that dollar with nostalgic memories of taking Danny to Sears to wander the tool aisle for fun, and trying to convince him to go to camp as if it were the first day, every day, this dollar was the only keepsake I had of our time together.

It would dawn on me much later that Danny's gesture may have also been his kid-boss way of tipping his house servant one last time before we said our goodbyes. Not so heartwarming after all, is it?

Danny did see himself as the boss. In fact, some of the only English he picked up from nine weeks in U.S. summer camp was, "I know all about it," paired with a flick of the wrist as if to shoo you away—a 6-year-old! I later decided to give this dollar, I mean my well-earned tip from my summer boss, to a homeless veteran. In that instant, I decided to re-name myself Rachel, or maybe Phoebe.

Just kidding.

I handed the dollar to the man on the corner and figured it could go further in his hand than in mine. It was, strangely, a small moment of release for me. I needed to let go of the worry I had for Danny and his development, his attachment issues, and life of being thrown around the world. I needed to accept my time with him for what it was: a drop in the bucket. A small moment in his life that may or may not have an effect on who he will become. Letting go is hard, and now when I reflect on my time with Monica and Danny,

I am so grateful this opportunity found me. You see, the time I spent with them was not just a drop in the bucket for me. Rather, it was a life-defining, formidable, and grounding experience that gave me confidence as a nanny, a future mother, and a woman.

He'll be fine, I told myself.

Maybe, one day, I'll get a friend request on Facebook from him and see him with his wife and kids, perfectly happy, says the lady with the rose-colored glasses.

CHAPTER FIVE

Gio, for Short

The next two weeks would surprise the hell out of me. I had only planned my summer up until Danny went back to China, so now that I was no longer Danny's nanny, who was I? Rather, what was I? Would I go back to working a normal job, and how long will it take me to get this job? I toyed with the idea of becoming an au pair and even got as far as filling out an application and getting a new passport photo. I was thinking Australia or maybe London, but after reading all the fine print and estimating what it would cost, I chickened out. I couldn't imagine going that far from home in Colorado, and I certainly couldn't afford a one-way ticket to Australia.

Without Danny, what was I doing here? I had this weird feeling, like when a person gets a limb amputated but the brain thinks it is still there. In my case, Danny was my missing limb. It felt like he should be with me, right there by my side, but suddenly he was not there anymore. I had only one week to figure out where I was going to go and what I was going to do. This was a fight or flight situation, and my fighter instincts were on high alert. I was adamant about finding a solution and determined to stay in Santa Barbara, no matter the scenario.

While camping out at my best friend Emily's house for a week, I feverishly started submitting applications on Indeed and scouring Craigslist and Care.com for side jobs to extend my stay. I had a few sketchy leads on places to live and made a short trip back to Colorado to regain my bearings.

I don't want to leave Santa Barbara. I feel like my journey is just getting started. It can't be over. I can't give up now. I convinced myself, and my mom, that something would work out.

I jump on a flight back to Santa Barbara to give it one last shot, and after only a few days, seemingly out of the clear blue sky, I got a job. A dermatology office hired me on the spot, and I was to start the very next Monday. No more crashing at Emily's. I had found a place to live as well. The whole thing felt like a Godsend, and like most things during this period of my life, I blindly walked into it all.

I found a room and moved in with ten Swedish people, one Dutch girl, one Serbian, and one girl from Palm Springs in a converted row home built in 1890. All of us had been coerced by the same Craigslist slumlord who owned a number of properties around town and charged an obscene amount of rent to non-suspecting European students—and me. The house was falling apart and we spent the first week recuperating from a flea infestation, but we were walking distance to the beach, and that was all we cared about.

I did my best at my new job but they let me go just shy of my 90-day probation period. It lasted long enough for me to get a few paychecks but not long enough for them to legally provide me with health insurance. How convenient for them.

According to the office manager, I suck at selling Botox, but to me, this was my "get out of jail for free card." I was miserable. The purpose I felt with Danny couldn't be matched. The office was suffocating. The people were vain, and simply put, I didn't care about what I was doing. I began looking for another nanny job. I was determined to find something.

In the middle of downtown Santa Barbara, living two steps from my favorite bar, I walked and biked everywhere, frequenting the beach as much as I could. Running amuck with Emily, my college dormmate who happened to live there too, I was happier than I had ever been. I knew however that this season of sunshine and rainbows was coming to an end.

I met some really horrible men and one really good one, before I painfully made the decision that it was now time to head back to Colorado. As I transitioned out of paradise, I spent my last month with one little man who would change my world forever— Giovanni Harris-Hughes Fallaguerradana—Gio, for short.

His parents are Lauren and Alex, who were some of the most refreshing people I met while in California. They weren't your average first-time parents. Lauren had her first child at 38 with Alex, who was almost 50. It was shocking for me to learn that Lauren's pregnancy was considered geriatric, because 38 didn't seem that old, I thought.

Gio was only 3 months old when I took care of him. While his original nanny was gone temporarily, I spent all day with him, and I had no idea what I was doing. "No, I don't know how to take care of a baby, Mom, but I can google it," I told my mom on the phone. Lauren had found me in the nick of time on Care.com, which I had been frantically skimming on an hourly basis since being fired from the Doctor's office.

I learned more than I ever thought I could about breast-feeding and pumping, teething, and napping. Gio was perfection, and Lauren ended up being my soul sister, inspiring me to calm down about settling down, showing me the fun that can be had before, during, and after marriage, all while having a baby. She was a liquor distributor, but that's a story for another time. Visualize this: a pregnant woman serving shots, or this: a woman driving across California each day with bottles of Jack stacked to the brim of her car and pumping while driving. Now, that's the modern mother. Heck yeah!

On the six-month-mark to the day, I got back in badass Black Betty and headed back to my land-locked fate. I mean the state of Colorado. The night before I left, I slept in my best friend's bed, which I had frequented nearly every weekend of that six-month-long summer. Feeling sorry for myself, and simply defeated by my decision to throw caution to the wind and move to the beach, I tearfully threw up my hands.

For the first time in my life, I didn't have a plan.

I didn't know why I was leaving, except for the elephant of unemployment in the room, or what I was going to do when I got back to Colorado. I was dreading my return.

At 25, I was exactly where I started—no job and still no money. I needed to grow up.

I sat on the beach for my last time, smoking half a cigarette I found floating in the bottom of my bag of paints. The energy of the waves matched my mood. I was being pushed and pulled by friends who were wanting to say goodbye and begging me not to go. As a people pleaser, this was not easy. To practice harnessing my impulsive nature, I opted to go to the beach alone with the intent to paint one last time at my favorite beachside spot.

My canvas was bare, and the paint bubble I had dolloped onto my palate was drying up. My mind was so preoccupied. I had filled out a simple application for an online master's degree program earlier that day, deciding, what the hell, I'm not getting into Stanford, so I might as well apply for this dinky program.

Well, to my surprise, I got in that very day. The email stated that I would start in two weeks. Though this immediate, and possibly automated response, signaled pure desperation on the school's part, I took it as a small win and signed up for my first few classes.

It didn't feel as glorious as I had imagined going back to school would be. The fog of self-doubt was creeping in. Like the tide, self-doubt had gradually come in since the job search began, and with each rejection, all my other life accomplishments were being taken out to sea, one by one, as if they didn't matter.

Because things on the job front were never working in my favor, the only way for me to feel in control was when I was in charge of my destiny. I got a high from making impulsive decisions, feeling excitement when I created problems that only I could solve for myself. I was more willing to take the risk if I was the only one who could get hurt in the process.

I needed my impulsive decisions to spring me back to life, to remind me that I am a fighter, to empower me. It was my upper, and I needed one last hoorah, so I packed up my paints and headed to the nearest tattoo parlor on State Street. If I was leaving Santa Barbara, I was going to leave with a parting gift to myself.

I settled on a simple magnolia flower. I had wanted this tattoo for a while and was finally ready to pull the trigger. This flower reminded me of playing in my grandmother's front yard in Arkansas, my favorite quote by Maya Angelou, and now, of Santa Barbara.

During my first bike ride in Santa Barbara, I had made a couple wrong turns and accidentally ended up on the west side of town. Biking down San Andres street, magnolias followed me for miles, making the most beautiful archway over my head. I remember gasping with awe at the number of flowers hanging above me. I had never seen this many before and, at that moment, I knew I wasn't lost at all. Rather the opposite. This was exactly where God intended me to be. Magnolias would later become God's way of whispering to me, confirming my direction, even when I was blindly led there.

At the tattoo parlor, I shed a few tears to accompany the pain of the needle, and as they dripped down the side of the leather tattoo chair, I released my final goodbye to my adventure in the sun. It was time to grow up and go home.

"I am convinced that most people do not grow up...We marry and dare to have children and call that growing up. I think what we do is mostly grow old. We carry accumulation of years in our bodies, and on our faces, but generally our real selves, the children inside, are innocent and shy as magnolias."

– Maya Angelou

CHAPTER SIX

The Long Way Home

Shit, wrong turn.

Shit, wrong turn again!

I swear that was the thousandth U-turn I had made in the last 15 minutes.

I had zero service in the desert. While Google Maps was continuously searching for connection, I grabbed the atlas that's been in my car for the past 10 years but never been opened. In my dad's send-off speech before my departure, he said, "You might need this one day. Always keep this in your car and cash in your wallet. You never know when shit might shut down." By "shit," he means the world, and by "shut down," he means what might happen if another Obama is in the White House.

I was such a jerk for rolling my eyes. I hate when he's right!

I was somewhere between Pasadena and Vegas. All I could see were miles of wind farms and translucent dust blowing across the vast span of highway. Where was I? It looked like Mars.

I knew I was going the right direction, but my unplanned detour had thrown me off. I had just stopped through Boron, California, a little tiny dot on the map. Boron was just a random California desert town, with a population of a little over 2,000 people. Surrounded by dry, arid landscape, it was perfect for the largest Borax mine in the world. This rural town is where Gio's mom, Lauren, had grown up, and I wanted to pay some homage, see her stomping grounds, and simply waste time.

I pulled over. Glancing at the atlas, I felt like an incompetent idiot who has never used anything but a cell phone to find her way. Finally placing my finger on the tiny Boron dot on the map, my phone rings.

"Oh, my phone is ringing! I must have service! Screw this atlas." I tossed it in the backseat and saw a number I didn't recognize on my screen.

"Hello?" I answered.

"Audrey, hi, it's Jenn. Your mom gave me your number. I know this is a little random, but I was hoping to talk to you about maybe nannying for me?"

"Oh, yeah, Jenn," I replied. "My mom said you might be calling. I'm actually driving back to Colorado right now. I'm on a little road trip from California."

"Oh, sorry to disturb you," Jenn said. "When will you be back?"

I didn't have a timeline exactly. I had nothing to get back to. I forced myself to say, "I'll be back sometime next week. I'll give you a call then and we can talk more."

The thought of putting this hard deadline on my trip was making me nauseous, and the idea of already jumping into nannying for another family did too. My mom was invited to Jenn's baby shower last month and had mentioned that I was nannying in California, but moving home to Colorado soon. My mom was constantly reminding me how important my job was. On days that I was feeling bored of stroller walks and naptime routines, she would give me one of her famous pep talks about how I was helping this family grow, keeping their baby fed and cared for while they worked, and it was the most important job in the world.

Now, I guessed my mom was pimping me out to nanny for her friends, which seems easier than scouring the internet for a job anyway.

Jenn said she was in need of a full-time nanny when she returns to work in a month. I hung up the phone and accepted my fate, feeling surprisingly relieved that a plan had basically been decided for me. I could focus on looking beyond the next few months of living at home and nannying giving me just enough time to get my feet on the ground, update my LinkedIn, yada, yada, yada.

I decided that until then, I am "Eat, Pray, Loving," channeling my inner Elizabeth Gilbert. How white can I be right now? As my first solo road trip, I intended for my week on the road to be full of contemplation, reflection, and a better idea of my life's direction.

Direction! I need directions!

Making one last U-turn, I headed back to I-15, going north to Vegas for the night. Eat, Pray, Love? More like eat gas station snacks, pray that I have cell service, and learn to love being alone.

With no plan to execute or purpose to hurry back to Colorado, I took the longest route possible to extend my independence and my wallet. Before this independent, self-sustaining woman officially moves back home to watch *The Bachelorette* every Monday night and drink wine with her mom, I mean roommate, I extended my adventure as long as I could without wiping out my checking account. At the time, the balance was under $300.00, and my savings was $45.38. I was told to always keep a little cushion in the savings account—key word: little.

I had planned to spend one night at the Grand Canyon. My car filled to the top, with my bike bouncing along through November rain and post-Thanksgiving fog, I arrived at the Grand Canyon right before sundown and spent two hours dangling my feet at the edge nearest the Visitors' Center. I sat there, taking deep belly breaths, trying to be present, overhearing a few urban travelers play some kind of flute and rainmaker in one of the cliff houses beneath my perch. Total cultural appropriation if you ask me, but I listened with a curious ear, imagining what these hippies were wearing and how it is that people literally convince themselves that they are native because their uncle is 1/23rd Cherokee.

I had never been to the big hole in the ground before, but before leaving Santa Barbara and after some late-night courage (i.e. Merlot), I had booked the cheapest single-cabin room with a shared community bathroom. I woke up to fog packed inside the Canyon like a thick custard, perfectly squeezed through the hole in a donut. The fog oozed out of some of the cracks and crevices, spilling onto the sides, where my feet met the same ledge I had sat on the night before.

It was disappointing. After years of only having interaction with nature and camping during Girl Scout trips, I got to spend only two hours at the Grand Canyon, or as they say, the big hole.

I need a donut.

Well, the show must go on, and as for me, my donut analogy had made me hungry. I checked the tethers on my bike and stopped at the gas station for breakfast on my way out of the park, headed towards Santa Fe, New Mexico. I planned for a seven- or eight-hour drive at most.

Thankfully, my aunt and uncle had a vacant condo where I could crash in New Mexico, as snowbirds do. They conveniently live at the beach in the winter, so I had the place all to myself.

Something strange happens to the mind when we move from one place to another. It's like the break you take between chapters in a book, when the chapter ends and sometimes you wait a week or two until deciding to start the next one. This break gives us time to think about what just happened. To reflect. We go over the details in our minds. Some might matter and some don't at all. We're trying to guess the end without knowing the whole story. As I took my time driving back home, a new sense of wonder and purpose fell upon my soul—or uterus—I'm not sure which one.

I thought about the past two experiences nannying. The families, the children, but also the meaning and the importance of being a mother, giving birth, giving life.

I had witnessed for my first time the purpose of why people get married, why we are meant for partnership while we are here on earth. Monica's husband was across the world, positioning her to be the only parent for her child, always accompanied by a nanny, of course. This explained Danny's consistent struggle with life on a daily basis. Throwing fits three times a day, acting as if he were the firstborn son of the Ming Dynasty. This estranged family dynamic, agitated by a 14-hour time difference and the added pressure of a baby ready to pop out, made me care so deeply for them, and especially little Danny.

On the other side of the fence, Lauren and Alex's refreshing take on marriage and family on their own terms left me feeling hopeful that I would someday have that in my own life.

After six months in the sunshine state, I was still terribly heartbroken from before I left. I was completely hung up on the same guy, thinking and feeling that I had lost a man that I may be meant to be with forever. As pathetic as that may sound, I was hoping this extended summer break would bring me a new life, but rather, I was returning home to my old life with nothing to show for it but a few tan lines.

Pulling into the driveway in Aurora, Colorado, I thought about how moving back into my parents' house would be social suicide. The feeling of utter defeat consumed me. No way would I let it bring me too far down. God had a plan for me that I would have never imagined for myself, and after I put Black Betty in park, I walked in the door to return once more to the time warp experience of living at home as a fully functioning adult.

In the depths of agony, I lay on my bed blankly staring at the highest point in the ceiling. This was the same spot I stared at after I failed geometry in ninth grade and was grounded for a summer, the same spot I stared a hole into every night after my best friend in high school moved away. Here I was, diving right back into the same habits. Sleeping in my childhood bedroom again sent me back in time. I was sulking, and it was pathetic.

Mustering up the gumption to nanny again meant I could avoid blindly scrolling through cyberspace for a job that I didn't want to do anyway. It seemed well worth it. I made a deal to be paid in cash and skip out on my taxes for a bit. I was going incognito. It sounds like a drug dealer, but the only other jobs that meet those criteria are ones that fall under manual or domestic labor. Other than reluctantly renewing my babysitter's club membership, and leaning on my parent's pocket books, I was only facing up to six months in a low-security facility in my parents' house. Six months at 26 years old might be social suicide, but it's not genocide. I'll live.

Something happens to your brain when you're forced to live in the same space as an adult where you also spent your adolescent years—too many hours calling the radio to request No Scrubs, downloading music on Napster. You suddenly embody your teenage self, and your parents are sent back into time to tag along with you arguing about cleaning your room, turning down your music, or remembering to lock the garage door at night.

I had been sneaking out to go to a bar, and sneaking back in, going to a "friend's house" for some wine and a "sleepover," aka hooking up with someone, and skipping church every Sunday because of "schoolwork." It was the lying that had me annoyed. I knew that "Living with the parents in your mid-twenties, Phase Two" was going to be a rough season and figured the best way to power through was to actually channel my younger self.

Just like my goal was in high school, I planned to be away from my house for as long as I possibly could. A lot of it had to do with Dad's drinking but it also had to do with Mom ignoring Dad's drinking. The Peter Pan shadow was prepared and ready for re-installation, but I had a plan—head down, work hard, move out.

I agreed to help Jenn full time, working 6:00 a.m. to 6:00 p.m. most days, with a little afternoon break. The strangest part, though, was being connected again to Jenn's family. You see, I thought this family was a thing of my past. I had been to college. I had been away from Aurora for years, and here I was working with some of the same people that knew me when I was in grade school.

Memories and visions of the past were soaking through my mind. Sleeping in my childhood bedroom didn't help, and I was looking for the exit sign already. Nothing about my childhood and how this family intersected with mine was something I wanted to remember. The Petersons were a family that shared so much with mine, and I was nervous about opening those flood gates of memories again.

Something tempting and lingering was waiting to submerse itself in my consciousness. I would face my past and resolve the angst I had with my teenage years by embracing the opportunity that had come my way. I needed to do the work to earn my future self and work towards who I wanted to be. I won't let the tide take out my accomplishments, but I will allow the gradual changes to take place and for some of them to fade away and make room for new ones.

I do not recall feeling like I was taking the bull by the horns and persisting, but as I look back on this time in my life, I know that's exactly what I was doing. I asked myself, "Do I want to be a person who mopes and groans at every pitfall, or a person who takes life by the diapers and sacrifices a few months of her twenties to help a fellow female who needs support?"

I was beginning to grasp what it meant to serve others, and I knew that Jenn needed me. She didn't need just any old nanny; she needed a friend, a partner, a woman who would truly help her fight. She chose me, and I chose her.

Head down, work hard, move out. Six months on the clock. Let's do this.

CHAPTER SEVEN

The Petersons and Me

The Petersons, Jenn's family of five, were very well-to-do. They were the perfect middle-class family. She and her siblings went to a good public school, and her father did some kind of number crunching. Her mom was one of those cool, born-again Christians. She belonged to a church that my family would later join as well, the type of church where you wear jeans and sing pop songs from a PowerPoint presentation. In fourth grade, I played softball with their youngest daughter and loved going over to visit their beautiful home. I never went over hungry though, because their mom was into granola, avocado, and rice cakes, while my mom was still taking me to McDonalds for the filet-o-fish because that was the healthy choice on the menu.

I grew up in the late 1990s, so, like a lot of white families in Aurora, everything was going pretty well. Free school meant more money for college, and though my schools were a little bit too diverse for my home-grown, Southern parents, I think we got a pretty good education. I mean, this was before educational standards existed, so there is no way to tell, said the girl who took pre-calculus four times and needed three attempts to pass her teaching exam.

As my seventh-grade class watched the twin towers come crashing down on a television perched in the highest corner of the room, that day would stand as one of the most significant days in my life. Things changed, and it was families like the Petersons, along with my own, that struggled behind closed doors. America was going to war, with talk of the Taliban and terrorists, Osama Bin Laden and George Bush, a young girl in her adolescence can only try to comprehend what this would mean for the future of her country, and wonder why her parents were always so stressed out.

My father is an airline pilot and had just been promoted to Captain at that time. He was asked to fill another role for the company. This role positioned him to furlough his fellow colleagues, witnessing firsthand their reactions of pain and extreme disbelief when he explained why they were being let go. Hearing stories of wives with cancer, children in college, and babies on the way, he could do nothing but explain the company's survival strategy, which included a massive cut in employees, pay, and benefits. As 401(k)s disappeared, airline rates skyrocketed, and college tuition became a dark burden, many middle-class families began to work more, drink more, take more anti-depressants, and pay less attention to the young people in their lives. It is the individuals who spent their adolescence in the early 2000s largely unsupervised and painfully mislead that make up most of the millennial generation today.

Infatuated with society, culture, poverty, social issues, and the current state of affairs for our country, I spent most of my time in high school dating boys my dad didn't approve of, performing with my dance squad at halftime to booty-poppin', misogynistic gangster rap, and avoiding my house at all costs. I'd like to think my experience isn't unique, that a lot of people had similar experiences.

Come to find out, a lot of people did, specifically, a lot of young women who were also nannying post-undergraduate school. According to the National Center for Educational Statistics, undergraduates who chose to major in a social science rose 16 percent in 2003 to 2009, and this number rose again by 40 percent from 2009 to 2014. This rise in social science popularity, combined with the financial crisis of 2009, was a perfect recipe for unemployment. In a place like Denver, Colorado, supposedly one of the most educated cities in America, competition was high, and for many folks, nannying seemed to be the only solution to this problem, due to quite a demand.

Jenn was the oldest of the three Peterson girls and had barely snuck by this timeframe. After graduating from the state college in the early 2000s, she settled down with a guy she had met at a friend's wedding. Unlike my friends and me, she met her husband in real life versus Tinder, Grinder, Bumble, and the list goes on. She got a great job with an oil and gas company a few years out of college and was well on track for what people claim to be a normal timeline:

1. Graduate from college

2. Meet a man

3. Get married

4. Have children before you're 30

Done.

The funky catch for Jenn was the geographical location at which her normal timeline played out. The man she married was from the Deep South, not a Florida or Texas kind of state. I'm talking an Alabama, Arkansas, Louisiana kind of state, where y'all is Ch'all and you've never heard longer vowels in everyday words. Where Chick-fil-A is the hottest spot in town and there are more churches in a square mile than fast food joints. You order a caramel Frappuccino, but you hear "Cara-mel Frap-AY" and the Home Depot sales associate matter-of-factly calls the insecticides area "the kill wall." Jenn was definitely far from white, crunchy-granola Colorado.

Coming from Denver to Jackson, Mississippi, was a far-left-field decision, but she described to me once how much the Southern culture had won her over. Her husband's family and her new friends had made her feel loved and welcomed. She adored that family, and enjoyed church being the center of everyday life. Plus, being a part of a large family gathered around food, fun, and music charmed her.

I understood the sentiment, as my entire extended family lives in Arkansas. My parents grew up in a tiny town surrounded by tall pines and muddy waters in the 1960s. Some places feel like a time capsule, stepping into a town that is still functioning and living like *Leave it to Beaver* or *The Andy Griffith* show. People wave at you when you pass them on the highway, and segregation is still in full effect, not by law of course, but just because you take the Whites Only sign off the door, doesn't mean it's any more inviting to people of color. Take out the white supremacy and Bible beaters, and the South certainly has a charm—the food, the twang, the drawl, you know, all the good parts.

Jenn had successfully won at life. Married at 24 and taking on the new last name of Moran, they started a family a year or so later, right on schedule. A year after giving birth to her first baby, Ava, Jenn and her husband, Brian, began to notice that Ava's hands would shake when grasping things. She wasn't walking quite yet, and they had enough concerns to take Ava to the doctor for some developmental exams.

Since the medical and research systems in Mississippi were still functioning in this time warp I described, a false diagnosis of rickets, the disease children in the 17th century acquired from a vitamin D deficiency, and some other failed attempts at identifying the mystery of Ava's condition, compelled Jenn to return to Colorado. This decision was made in spite of the fact that she had just learned she was pregnant for the second time and that her husband had to stay in Mississippi to run his businesses. She would be pregnant and alone, with her baby who was nearing 2 years old and was fighting a mysterious illness she couldn't even name.

Frightened, anxious, and scared, Jenn was channeling her mama bear-ness, stopping at nothing to find out what was going on with Ava, even if it meant throwing her perfect timeline out the window. In Colorado she could be closer to her parents and have access to some of the best doctors and physicians in the nation. At eight months pregnant, Jenn moved to Colorado and, soon thereafter, gave birth to her second child, this one with a Colorado birth certificate.

It was at this exact moment in time, November 2014, that I was on the first leg of my road trip back to Colorado. In the middle of nowhere, in the California desert just beyond Joshua Tree, I took a wrong turn and answered her call.

After speaking with Jenn that day, I couldn't help but try to understand what she was going through. She was in for the long haul, with a newborn and a two-year-old. The fact that Ava was not walking or talking on her own was an added layer of distress. Without a partner there to help on a daily basis, it was no wonder she needed an extra hand! If only I were an octopus, because that's how many extra hands she realistically needed. My role as her nanny was so much more than that. I could list off all the things I did for her over the next six months, but I would rather tell you the things she did for me.

Jenn is a mom who woke up every morning way before her children's biological alarm clocks went off to clean up the bathroom, throw in some laundry, run the coffee machine, and start work, all before 6:00 am, when I would arrive. If you know anything about the biological alarm clocks of babies and 2-year-olds, well, let's just say their bodies are set on a four-hour reminder mode that you can never turn off.

Her energetic willingness to pursue each day was the most inspiring thing I have ever seen. I was astonished daily by the amount of gumption and drive this woman had, despite all the challenges and setbacks she experienced each time she had to make a claim with the insurance companies, or when another test result came back without answers. She is an extraordinary example of what it means to be a mother.

For the next six months, I watched Jenn wake up every morning, get to work at her desk next to the laundry machine, breast-feed almost every five minutes, take calls from doctors, nurses and insurance agents, all in between work meetings.

Even in the midst of racing out the door to get someone to school or to a doctor's appointment, she was always singing, playing, and laughing with her children. I often found myself thinking, "How the hell does she do it?" Sure, I picked up a lot of the slack, ran the dishwasher sometimes, picked Ava up from school, took her to appointments, and put the baby down for a nap, but in no way did I feel as though I was her "help."

In part, some of this equality I felt between myself and Jenn came simply from our similar demographics. Both college-educated, white, Democratic women from Colorado and similar in age, we had a lot in common. Often talking about politics, education, history, and current events, we enjoyed one another's company and became closer than the typical nanny-mom relationship. She knew I was helping out not because I intended to make nannying my career or because nannying was the role of my foremothers, but because I was in a post-graduate, high-unemployment-rate bind. This leveling of the power structure between worker and supervisor, nanny and matriarch, enabled us to become friends. We compared stories about our similar families and interests, her past dating experiences and my current, very single existence.

Jenn is taller than average, but not Amazonian, a good five feet, 10 inches, perhaps. She was that perfect combination of slender and toned, with a natural tan only a Swedish descendant could have. She enjoyed the occasional four-to five-mile bike ride along the creek's edge near the house, though it was rare to steal away an hour of time, but she made it a point to eat healthy and be active. The way she lived her life was refreshing to me, and perhaps too perfect, as Jenn was clearly an overachiever, but being a perfectionist when it comes to motherhood, and life in general, isn't such a bad thing.

It's called survival, and Jenn was surviving her every day with grace, agility, and pure adrenalin (i.e. coffee).

I felt as though this was the most reciprocal experiences I had ever had as a nanny. What I was learning from Jenn was a devout passion and focus on what's most important to her: family. On the rare occasion that her husband was able to visit, I was also able to see what an important and steadfast relationship they had. Though time and space separated him from his wife, daughter, and newborn baby, I was able to see and witness a relationship that was healthy and strong in the face of extreme circumstances, and at times, extreme sadness.

As the family began to meet with more specialists and conduct more tests, they realized that Ava would likely never move or speak in the way we see as normal. Despite this monumental realization and the magnitude of how their daughter's life would forever affect their lives, they always had an optimistic outlook on what Ava would be capable of doing one day. With the financial resources this family had, the spectrum of therapies were limitless. Without financial constraint, families with children with disabilities can access everything from equestrian therapy to special camps and opportunities for their children. You can say this family is certainly blessed, and though having a child with a disability can be challenging no matter how rich you are, it is undeniably true that money softens the blow.

Working with families and children through the public schools and nonprofit programs, nothing is more eye-opening than seeing how the needs and the resources available do not match up. Even for a woman who is of financial ability to afford special programs, it was still an immense struggle to find a public school that met Ava's needs. This, like many other topics with childcare, constantly leave me wondering—what do families do who cannot afford it? Reflecting back on our parents, who had been fired or demoted in the midst of the 2008 stock market crash, they were indeed doing the best they knew how. I saw unlikely people coming together to carpool to make sure we didn't miss dance class or the student council camp. The Petersons had been there for me and my family growing up, and now ironically, it was my turn to help one of them.

CHAPTER EIGHT

Whiteness—Check!

As an ethnic studies major (aka unemployable), I learned a consciousness ritual called "confronting my whiteness" during my time in undergraduate school. This is something I learned in my liberal, hippy college courses I attended at the University of Colorado-Boulder. This place suffered from a bad case of trust funds, lots of pot smoking, and a 94.6 percent Caucasian student population with no Hispanic or Latino background. I had found myself at possibly the whitest place on the planet. Though I myself am white, blonde, and upper-middle-ish class, I was somehow still able to feel like the odd woman out. In a sea of fake tans, Ugg boots, fraternity keggers, skiing, and rock climbing, I found myself seeking out places that held any kind of racial and cultural diversity, because it literally couldn't have been whiter.

As ethnic studies became my home, amidst red-shirted football players who needed an easy 'A' to young women of color who were on their way to becoming badass Ph.D. scholars, I was usually one of the few white people in the room, and to my Southern father's dismay, this was just the way I liked it.

In my last year of school, I was completing my final project in a research methods class. My professor was Native American/American Indian, two-spirited[3] and definitely a politically

---

[3] Two-Spirit is a modern, pan-Indian, umbrella term used by some Indigenous North Americans to describe Native people in their communities who fulfill a traditional third-gender (or other gender-variant) ceremonial role in their cultures. (Wikipedia, March 2020)

correct word Nazi. They blew my mind every class. It was rigorous and it was painful. That year, I learned what it looks like, and what it sounds like, to confront racism, not to just figuratively or philosophically confront it when you are talking politics at a bar, but to do it in real life. I learned what it will take for our society and our world to make some serious social changes, and it confirmed my passion for wanting a career that helps to make that change.

The lesson that made the biggest impact for me was titled: "Checking Your Whiteness." At first, my white fragility stood in the way of truly analyzing my own privileges, admitting that I too, was a part of the problem. I realized that the only way I would be able to make a difference is to help other white people learn what I had learned. I ruffled a few feathers that year, especially with my parents and my friends. It was hard for people to understand why a white girl cared so much. But from my side of the table, I couldn't understand why they didn't. Being white conveniently gave people the ability to easily opt out of talking about race and racism, but I was running straight into these conversations, even when it was uncomfortable.

To check one's whiteness is to consciously think about how my white privileges, along with my class, sexuality, gender, age, and more play a significant role in how I experience situations, relationships, even my feelings towards my own life. This practice has been pivotal in my reflection of my life, my experience post-graduate school, and how I see the world around me. I'm trying my best to be a woke white girl by stayin' up on social justice trends via Instagram and sharing CNN news stories on Facebook, but as we all know, that is not enough to make real change.

When it comes to analyzing my friendship with Jenn, which was formed despite the fact that I was technically her subordinate and she my superior, I knew that if I were of a different race, gender, age, sexuality, etc., this friendship may have not formed in the way it did. I mean come on. If I were a black, homosexual, elderly man

—the opposite of what I am—this would have been a completely different story, and would potentially be a best-selling book.

Anyway, the way Americans relate to one another is not always clear. I mean, using the N-word in 2018 while watching Klan members defend their precious confederate statues is clearly messed up, but if you're one of the many who function in the multicultural and globalized world and have any understanding of the meaning of privilege, some of our preconceived notions or perceived understandings of one another are not too clear.

It's like we're looking through smudged glasses that need to be cleaned. On the other side of the lens are two people standing at a bus stop, but that smudge is perfectly blocking your vision from seeing one of those people clearly; therefore, we have to assume that those people might be two men, standing next to one another waiting for the bus. Maybe they're strangers. Maybe they're family, possibly not too wealthy since they're taking the bus, or maybe they are environmentalists. That smudge is made of our subconscious thoughts about race, culture, class, sex, gender, lifestyle, and age, whatever. It depends how much you're willing to put into cleaning your glasses to look past the smudge and see what is really in front of you. Putting aside our assumptions and preconceived notions and bias is nearly impossible. We are products of our environments. If poor people take the bus, then the people waiting for the bus must be poor, right?

What I learned from this mean professor in college was that on a daily basis I must check my preconceived ideas that I have about others. Checking my whiteness goes beyond the general understanding of racism. It's more than not saying the N-word when I sing along to my favorite Tupac song with my other white friends in the car. It goes beyond the racial politics that we see in the news, or liking a Black Lives Matter post, and appreciating Beyoncé's latest album that highlights the African diaspora and complexity of the African-American experience.

Race and the history of race in America is embedded in our American consciousness and how we see other people as "other" people. How we experience our lives today is connected directly to our many histories. It is what fuels institutionalized racism and explains the incarceration rates of black men in our country today. Our histories give validity to the Black Lives Matter Movement, and make the All Lives Matter movement a freaking joke.

As I write this chapter, it is the beginning of the Trump presidency, and racism in America seems to be more prevalent than I ever thought it could be in the 21st century. I had another professor claim once that "we will know when real progress has been made, when we see white students at CU protesting about the lack of diversity on campus." So along this same line of argument, it will not be until every white family discusses race around their dinner table with their kids that race will finally become something we understand, we respect, we confront, and we love. It's not until then that we can move forward from the horrors and travesty of slavery—not to forget—but to begin to rebuild the America we all want to believe in.

The history of women of color as caretakers, nannies, maids, and house slaves alongside the history of white women being their superiors, is the history that specifically has impacted my life. I'm not saying that if I were Black, that Jenn and I wouldn't have a relationship, but what I am saying is that if I were Black, Jenn and I would have a different relationship. It is so important to highlight this whiteness, because as I moved forward in my journey as a nanny for seven more babies through my mid-twenties, I came to believe that the evolution of the nanny position, and how it has shifted over time from predominantly low-income women of color to now young white women, highlights a real example of white privilege that is worth talking about.

PART II

CHAPTER NINE

The South's Warmest Welcome

January through April in Colorado is always really crappy, especially when you have a two-wheel drive car and don't have a snow sport to keep you occupied all winter and spring. I survived it though. I made it to April 7, 2015, my 26th birthday.

Even though I was wishing Obama had cared more about those of us who still needed mommy and daddy's insurance coverage at 26, I updated my LinkedIn profile and had finally landed a job with a charter school in Denver Public Schools. I soon learned that I had been chosen to teach eighth grade language arts later that fall in northwest Denver. It was in a neighborhood I knew nothing about, and though I was a total newbie with no teaching license, I was stoked to rise to the challenge. Charter schools are like startups for the education sector. We were not sure how long some of them would last, but they were suddenly hiring like crazy.

This gave me three more months with Jenn, Ava, and the baby, and I decided I could deal with that. This was summer, 2015, one full year after my Santa Barbara adventure.

Each day I arrived at Jenn's, I was in for a surprise.

She's clearly running behind and greets me in one exasperated breath. "Hey Audrey, so glad you're early. The baby is sleeping. It sounds like Ava is awake, but just barely. I need to shower and get on a call in 25 minutes. Are you good?"

"Totally," I reassure her, and she is on her way, speed-racing to the shower.

I spend the next 15 minutes putting my stuff down and listening to Ava rustle around in her crib. I take a look at the monitor and, of course, see her standing straight up. With a death grip on the guardrail of the bed and another hand wiping her hair out of her face, she begins to make various noises, knowing I will eventually poke my head in to come get her. Steadily, she gets louder, so I take a deep breath and chug the coffee that Jenn had poured for herself yet left for me to finish, and grab Ava from her bed.

I place her in front of the tube. She is hardly awake enough to start telling me what she wants; therefore, I have at least 10 more minutes to think of what's next: breakfast, filling a sippy cup with milk and putting some dry Cheerios in a bowl. I try to get this in front of her as soon as possible. The faster I think of what she wants before she knows she wants it, the less time I spend listening to her cry and whine about things she wants. Like with any toddler, I have to stay three steps ahead in order to get anything done.

As soon as Jenn is out of shower, we are off to the races. At 6:20 a.m., the baby emerges with Jenn from the back bedroom. She hands him off to me and is already on her first call of the day. While she unloads the dishwasher, she puts her call on mute, turns on the speaker phone, and places her phone on the counter so she can keep moving. Meanwhile, I am picking up Cheerios Ava has dropped on the floor while balancing the baby on my hip.

Most of Jenn's clients were on the east coast, making her work day start around 7:00 a.m. Denver time, with the exception of a 6:15 a.m. call that she had at least once a week. This was that type of day.

Jenn puts in her headphones so she can have her call handsfree and takes the baby so she can breastfeed. Placing her call on mute again, she updates me with what Ava needs to take with her to school and we exchange plans for the day. Jenn has meetings all morning, but we do the math, and when I return from dropping Ava at school, the baby can eat again by 9:00 a.m., so we should be good to go.

I change and dress Ava while Jenn breastfeeds on the couch and answers whatever questions her boss is throwing her way. Mornings like this feel like we are doing a synchronized dance, it's never a perfect routine but the key is that we keep moving. I head out the door by 7:30 a.m. with the baby and all the crap that comes with him, and Ava and all the crap that comes with her. Off we go!

In odd moments I feel important and accomplished as I load the car with Ava in her car seat, goldfish crackers and iPad entertaining her while I run back to grab the baby in his carrier and Ava's walker. On a good day, no one is crying and everything goes smoothly, but that is about a one-in-five-day chance. Crying or not, pretending to be a mom certainly gives me this feeling of excitement and purpose, almost like their lives are in my hands, and maybe because they are—kind of hero-esque, or should I say shero-esque?

When I pull out of the driveway in Jenn's car, not exactly a mom car but an SUV that fits all things kid-related, I feel a sense of freedom. The little ones are buckled in, essentially trapped and safe, so therefore I am free. I turn on music and look in the rearview to catch a glimpse of what Ava is up to. My favorite moments are when she happens to care less about the iPad and she is looking back at me in the rearview mirror. We jam out to the radio, me reaching back to tickle her feet at the red lights. The baby hangin' tight, usually making no more than a few peeps. I learned to pray that he doesn't fall asleep before we get to school. Nothing is worse than waking a sleeping baby. I contemplate leaving him in the car just for a minute, but every time, my integrity kicks in and I am waking him up to drag him and the 20-pound carrier into the school along with Ava and all the rest of her stuff.

It takes me a total of five minutes to get Ava out of her car and into the school. This is a ridiculously long amount of time, seeing how the school has a drive-up and drop-off lane in which you can get your car within four feet of the front door. It's supposed to be easy, but with Ava's disability, everything is a battle. Trying to gracefully dip and hoist her 27-pound body onto my hip while grabbing her bag, the baby, and his carrier, I close the door with my free butt cheek and double-check that I have the car keys in my hand.

These weren't my kids, so there's no question. I couldn't leave the baby in the car, even on the cold days when I knew it would be fine, I still never did it. That feels like a messed-up nanny-success of sorts, but it's the truth. I drop off Ava and the baby with a teacher in the lobby and walk back to get Ava's 20-pound walker. I return in seconds, trade the walker for the carrier, thank the teacher, and head back to the car. By the time this is all done, I am sweating buckets.

After dropping Ava off, I would take the long way home, trying to ride out the baby's nap, which always had its onset in the car. Arriving back home, the baby was famished, crying out in desperation as I handed him off to Jenn at 9:00 a.m. Though the afternoons were much calmer, every three to four hours Jenn would come to the living room to breastfeed, and I would take walks with the baby, listen to NPR podcasts, put the baby down for naps, and do school work in between.

Just when things started to feel repetitive, I'd get a wake-up call. With kids and life in general, it's only a matter of time before a curve ball is thrown your way. Learning to dodge, duck, and act quick on my feet was all a part of being a nanny. My time was always at the will of others, Ava's will, the baby's will, Jenn's and her job. Flexibility was the key to success, and letting go of any control I thought I had over my own work schedule was the only coping mechanism I had.

By December 2015, I had already changed my master's program twice, like any millennial would do. I was feeling like I was probably getting myself somewhere. Probably. It seemed to help, as I was just offered my first job in more than three years, and this one actually offered insurance, so that had to mean something, right?

Jenn was excited for me, though the frightening thought of me leaving her was hard for her to hide. A new plan had developed for her as well. Colorado was no longer a place she could be. The family needed to be together, and the only option was to return to Mississippi. My last month with the Moran family was spent in a place that frankly is worse than Arkansas—Mississippi. In the middle of the summer heat, Jenn and I packed up the boxes, all the kids' stuff, our own luggage, and with whatever brain power was left, we traveled back in time—back to Mississippi. We joked that her son would be confused, thinking he had two moms because his first six months of life had been spent mostly with his mom and me. I had finagled co-parenting with Jenn, and figured one last month helping her settle back into her life in the South was my final, selfless nanny-gift to the world.

Since this was my first traveling experience with young children, I now have a reminder that we should always feel bad for the mother with the crying baby on flights and have sympathy for the dad who has to chase his toddler up and down the aisle to avoid a claustrophobic tantrum. The route was lengthy, leaving Denver in the wee hours of the morning to land in New Orleans, rent a car and travel three more hours to the Magnolia State where the state slogan stands as the South's Warmest Welcome. I'd say 97 degrees with 100 percent humidity is a little more than warm.

Finally, when I got into bed that night, I was compelled to write something down. Thankfully, for the purpose of this book, I kept up with journaling while I was in Mississippi for a full two days. I am not much for routine. I try, but it usually goes south really quick; no pun intended.

The purpose of my journaling ritual was to help me document my memories but it wasn't long until my journaling turned into longhand notes and lists of random things I witnessed over my 30 days in Mississippi.

Mississippi Day 1

I got here after flying from Denver to New Orleans with Ava, the 3-year-old with special needs, Martin, the 6-month-old baby, and Jenn, the mom. We had to drive three hours from New Orleans and dropped off the rental car at the airport in Jackson, Mississippi, before heading to their new home in the suburbs. Jenn had only seen this house one time before, and Brian, the dad, was currently unloading the 18-wheeler moving truck. After changing 300 poopy diapers, we finally returned the car to the rental place and were picked up by the grandparents, who are the most quintessentially Southern people I've ever met.

Jenn and Brian bought this massive mansion in a gated community. It's really nice, and thankfully I have my own room and bathroom on the other end of the house from the kids and the parents. Good deal per my living quarters, so that was nice; though I literally worked 12 hours yesterday, so that was tiresome!

Mississippi Day 2

I compiled notes from my time in Mississippi:

- Jenn forgot her wallet in the rental car. Lucky me, I went to get it. It seemed like an adventure until I realized I was in Mississippi.

- I went to Home Depot. The man standing next to me in line wasn't wearing shoes. NBD.

- The sales associate called the area for the bug and insecticides the "kill wall"- [Keel wahl].

- Chick-fil-A seems to be the most popular place in the world. The line was out to the street at 9:30 a.m. and again at 2:30 p.m. and 7 p.m.

- They had so many Styrofoam cups! Don't these people know how bad that is for the environment?

- Sugarrrr, Carahmel frappay—how the hell do you phonetically spell that?

- While studying at a coffee shop, I noticed some nursing students. All four of them had the same outfits: faded neon, oversized sorority t-shirts, swishy running shorts, and Tivas. Are they hiking somewhere?

  Two boys just walked in. They have the same outfits on as the nursing students, but change the shorts to khakis.

- Yes, monogramed casserole dishes are a thing.

- I asked, "What's in this salad?" The woman replied, "Just some dressing." Mayonnaise is dressing?

- I had a Tinder date, but he canceled because his "boat broke." Then, when I met up with him, he had a black eye. He sounded just like Bill Clinton. I Ubered home.

- I went to Jackson State University to attend my high school friend's Zumba class. It's the most booty poppin' Zumba class I've ever done and I highly recommend it. The campus police officer stopped me in the parking lot after class asking, "Excuse me miss, are you lost?" This was a joke, as he was clearly making fun of the fact that a white girl was walking around a historically Black college, at night, in downtown Jackson, Mississippi. Though I didn't feel unsafe, he insisted on driving me to my vehicle.

- I got asked out by Oliver Black. When he asked me if I knew who he was and I said no, he claimed to be 49th in the country in track and that I should google him. I did. Two thumbs up, but Oliver, I don't care.

- The male dance squad at Jackson State was perfection with a side of absolute fabulousness!

- I got an invitation to a car show when I went to Zumba. This cute little sophomore added me on Instagram and told me to come find her at the show. She said, "Look for the Impala with the pink eye lashes and rims." I didn't make it, but her Instagram is real entertaining—so many belfies.[4]

- The best neighborhood was Fondren, a hipster gentrified neighborhood in Jackson. *The Help* was filmed there. It's also the only place in Mississippi I could find a yoga studio.

- The best night ever was when I went to the Mississippi beer festival with a couple Jenn used to work with. Obviously, Mississippi is new to the whole beer festival thing because they had the tallest pours and everyone was smashed in the first hour. That night I slept at this couple's house, where their black lab had given birth to 10 puppies a week prior—heaven.

It was the best of times. It was the worst of times, and soon enough my 30 days were up. I tearfully hugged and kissed my dear friend and her precious kids who had started to feel like my own. Goodbye. There I was, a little less than a year after leaving California, back in the car. Annoyingly, it wasn't Black Betty but

---

[4] Belfie: a "bottom selfie." A photographic self-portrait featuring the buttocks, usually posted by female celebrities on social media networks.

rather a rental. This time I was coming from the South looking forward to my nicely laid out plan in Colorado. I was stoked.

CHAPTER TEN

Goodbye

As I reflect on my short-lived experiences being a nanny, especially when I compare my experience to those before me, my experience was not a struggle in any way. Struggle is not relative when you contextualize it. Sure, I am pissed I had to live with my parents for so long and feel like I am using my bachelor's degree to drive kids to school and attend Mommy and Me music classes, but my struggle cannot be compared to those who have come before me. It's not so relative when I think about the women who have nannied out of necessity and for survival. I have replaced and out-qualified nannies of color, especially the elderly nannies of color who are still working their tails off in the Deep South today.

My generation of young, millennial, college-educated, mostly white women have displaced a demographic from a role that once was the only position a woman of color could have. From house slave, to wet nurse, to maid and nanny, the caretaker position has evolved and withstood the test of time. To quote an old and well-known saying, it certainly does take a village to raise a child.

When the family moved back to Mississippi, it became a reality that I was soon going to leave them. Jenn was forced to replace me.

When Ava was a newborn, she had a Nanny in Mississippi who cared for her. Marcie was an elderly black woman, born and raised in Vicksburg, Mississippi. She had nannied for a number of families before Ava, and her entire career was being a nanny for white families in town. Just like her mother passed down the job to her, her daughters were just beginning their lives as nannies as well.

Marcie was an expert at not only taking care of babies, but also in meandering through the everyday lives and homes of white families. Jenn loved Marcie. Marcie was caring and sweet and taught Jenn so much about caring for an infant. As Ava grew bigger and stronger, but still unable to mobilize on her own, the job was very taxing on Marcie, and Jenn could tell it was becoming difficult for her to keep up. Given her age and Ava's situation, it was very difficult for Marcie to give Ava the care she needed.

Going back to Marcie or hiring another elderly individual as Ava's caretaker was simply not an option. Ava now weighed nearly 30 pounds and required physical assistance at all times.

As we scrolled through Care.com and weeded through her friends' suggestions and connections, we both agreed that Mississippi had slim pickings from the nanny pot. Elderly women, predominantly African American, who had nannied their entire lives, were too old. Young girls who dropped out of high school to carry on the family nannying business were too inexperienced to work with Ava. Not finding a qualified replacement made Jenn increasingly nervous.

I remember Jenn describing the time that Marcie spent with her in her home when Ava was just born. "It was odd. I felt like I was living in the past, like I was witnessing some of the stuff the movie *The Help* was about, but it was 2013!" Jenn had been raised in Colorado, and without this cultural and historical knowledge, it seemed a bit of a culture shock to live this life in the Deep South where it was normal to have "help."

Eventually, Jenn found a nanny, a 22-year-old woman, a military wife with fake boobs and a mouth that went 5,000 words a minute. She was no Audrey, and ended up quitting after 5 months, relocating with her military husband to Texas.

Change is not easy for Ava, as it isn't with any toddler. Moving back to Mississippi in a new house, with a new nanny soon to leave, Jenn was at her wit's end trying to keep up, again faced with the stressful decisions that involved care for the most important people in her life, her children.

She was caught, like most women are in the 21st century, between working and being a mom. It is a dream-like fantasy to imagine this decision being easy for any woman. We go to school. We get degrees. We work. We have kids, and then we are torn— torn between the calling of motherhood, to raise our kids, and spend every waking moment with them, while wanting to pursue our careers, and use our creative and intellectual capacities as humans to contribute to the world.

I spent $100.00 shipping my months' worth of clothes back to Denver. I packed like I was prepared to live a year abroad. I had only 24 hours left in Mississippi and I wondered if I would ever return. Odds are I won't. Maybe to visit Ava, but it's very likely I will never go back. I had rented a little car, ironically a red Ford Focus, Black Betty's red-headed cousin, and planned to meet my college roommate for a Fourth of July girl's trip to Nashville. Before embarking on this solo road trip and break from my celibate Mary Poppins existence. I had to do what I had been dreading since the beginning; say goodbye.

Jenn had been prepping Ava for my departure for the last few days. When I entered her room, she playfully yelled and screamed at me, thinking I was trying to play or wrestle with her, but I picked her up out of her bed and held on to her tight. We sat on the floor of her bedroom together, her in my lap. I said, "Ava, I love you. You are such a good girl, so strong. I'm going to miss you. I am going to leave but I know I will see you soon."

I immediately regretted saying that. I don't know when the hell I am going to see her next, and I was already feeding her false hope and breaking her heart. This was so tough.

Ava said my name as she put her whole body weight into hugging me back. The way she said my name sounded a little like "ahhh-eeee." Her tongue, unable to make the sounds she intended for it, changed her words into unrecognizable alliterations, but I was well-versed in Ava's language after six months. I think about how hard it will be for the next girl. "Ahhh Eee." That's how my youngest sister said my name when she was 1 year old or so, so innocent, so pure.

Ava saw my tears and hugged me back, relaxing her erratic and uncontrollable ataxia movements and sinking into my lap. She knew I was leaving. She knew I was saying goodbye. The thing with Ava is that she is just like any typical three-year-old—stubborn and silly, sweet and demanding. The only difference is a second or two delay when her body would respond to her brain's directions. She would reach for something, like when it's dark outside and you're reaching in your backseat for your bag but you're too lazy to actually turn the light on and turn around to look for it first. You reach out and hit everything else before you finally grasp the bag. She would usually miss the first two times, but as persistent as she was, she eventually grabbed whatever she was reaching for.

That's Ava, for you, never giving up. At 5 years old, she would finally take her first consecutive 15 steps without assistance—holding her elbows tight to her sides, clenching her fists, controlling her shaking legs to merely keep herself balanced on her own two feet—and we complain when the Pilates teacher says, "Engage your core!" This little girl has a miniature six pack. It is truly incredible the strength and willpower she activates with every single step.

Ataxia is often something people acquire over time. Usually adults who have abused alcohol for years or experienced a brain injury will have "the shakes" which is how ataxia is commonly described. This is the mystery behind Ava's condition, and the core of the frustration and despair it has caused her parents. They have been unable to point to any moment in utero or infancy that could have caused her cerebellum to be so underdeveloped. In Colorado, Jenn was able to find doctors who would conduct genetic testing, trying to pinpoint what caused Ava to have what the doctors call "cerebral atrophy."

It was their desperation to answer the question that brought Jenn with her newborn baby and Ava to Colorado. Why does Ava have this? What went wrong? Did something happen in utero that they didn't know about? How was Jenn's diet during pregnancy? Did Ava fall off the bed and hit her head when she was an infant?

All of these questions certainly pained Jenn and Brian to the point of desperation. I cannot tell you what I would have done in their situation.

Even witnessing firsthand Jenn's daily struggles as a mom of two without her husband, facing one of the most difficult moments of her life, I can hardly imagine what she must have felt.

What shocks me is how she took every adversity, every moment of frustration, and handled it with grace. Though she would likely never agree with me, Jenn is most certainly what I call a Supermom. Forever I will be inspired by her fearlessness and will to carry on. She has proven to me that we, as women, can do anything. Tough times will continue, and we carry through with grace and poise, ready for the next challenge.

Jenn and I were always in Superman mode, watching every move Ava made, ready to catch her the minute she lost her balance. Before she would catch the corner of a coffee table, we were able to avoid the occasional goose egg or raspberry, but not all of the time.

This goodbye was not like any other goodbye I have ever made. It reached the furthest point on my goodbye meter. It was worse than the leaving for college goodbye, worse than the break up goodbye, and way worse than my Danny-land goodbye. To witness the everyday life of another person is powerful. It gives you perspective. It makes you feel grateful for what you have. Jenn's struggle is not the same as any other person's struggle. It is uniquely her own as is Teen's experience and mine.

I tearfully carried Ava to her mom, hugging them both and trying to pick up the mood with a few funny comments. I was feeling the anxiety of getting in the car and trying to avoid breaking into sobs. I told Jenn I would text her as soon as I arrived in Nashville, and watched Ava and Jenn wave goodbye in the rearview mirror.

CHAPTER ELEVEN

On the Road Again

Again, there I was. With a mixture of freedom and sorrow, I stopped at the first gas station and purchased a pack of cigarettes to accompany me on my way out of Magnolia-town. Smoking had now become a nasty habit of mine, primarily intensified when I was stressed, or bored. I found it successful in subsiding the urge to bite my nails. I knew it wasn't good, but it was better than my Dad's chosen poison, so I'll take it.

Between drags I looked for a station on the radio to keep me from crying more. Willie Nelson and Johnny Cash were singing *On the Road Again*. I just laughed to myself, "Like a band of gypsies rolling down the highway." I was feeling like a nomad, a vagabond or traveler. I had moved every six months for the past five years and put 30,000 miles on my car as well. Here I was again, leaving another family behind to fend for themselves. At the time, I truly felt like there could be no way they could survive without me. Who's going to be patient with Ava when she wants to do something by herself? Who is going to listen to Jenn and comfort her worries about doctor's appointments and insurance claims?

Letting go was not easy. I still felt an overwhelming sense of maternal ownership over the baby's sleeping patterns.

About an hour into my second solo road trip of my life, I settled down, feeling excited for a trip to Music City. My thoughts and feelings were flying all over the place. Maybe it was the coffee and cigs, but as I have now learned about myself, long transitionary car rides call for reflection, leading to contemplation, oftentimes leading to worry.

I had made it. My six-month basic-mom training was over, but something was still hanging in the air, something I was running from, or actually, someone I was trying hard not to focus on. I had taken another long way home back to Colorado. This time, things were actually looking up for me. I had found a studio apartment on Craigslist in my $700.00 per month price range. I was a little over halfway through my online graduate classes, ready to teach eighth grade English, visualizing *Freedom Writers*, embarrassingly so, and supposed to be feeling complete, right? I was ready to move in, but the reason I left Colorado in the first place would be closer than ever and I was determined to not let my former boyfriend tarnish my newfound *Sex in The City*-inspired life in Downtown Denver's edgiest hipster neighborhood.

After too many nights of silence and never a text or a call, I had the feeling it wasn't going to happen. I reached out two nights prior to my departure in an email. "It is all or nothing," I wrote.

It was a little extreme. I likely let myself suffer in silence for too long, writing this email in the heat of the moment and scrunching my face and eyes squeezed tight before hitting send. It was daring, but it felt good. I had nothing to lose. I had to place the ball in his court completely. I was going crazy and it was the only thing I could think about.

Should I have written him that e-mail?

What the hell was I thinking?

He's going to give that e-mail one little look and run for the hills.

Good going.

Why do I have to be so intense sometimes, so emotional and impulsive?

You know what? Screw him if he doesn't respond. This is it, the last straw, I swear. I am done playing games. It's been a year and a half of nothing. He gives you an inch before you left for Mississippi and you take a mile. You asked for it, and you knew exactly what you were getting into.

Why can't I let it go? Why do I feel so certain he is the one? You can't be serious.

Am I delusional, ridiculously blind to the signs he gives me of being uninterested and noncommittal?

We do have energy—this atmospheric synergy between us. He is the best man I know. He has so much potential, and I know he has to be the person I am supposed to be with.

My hands were thrown in the air though.

Feeling like I had nothing to lose, I returned my rental car and took an Uber to the hostel where I was to meet Emily—the same ex-college roommate, same bestie from Santa Barbara. We stayed in the Joni Mitchell room, and shared bunk beds with two other girls, both traveling solo for the Fourth of July holiday. We enjoyed the usual binge drinking, Fourth of July fireworks show and a random El Salvador versus USA soccer game with our hostel roommates, and more.

The minute I started enjoying myself, I'd be reminded of the awkward silence since I had clicked send. Feeling a little dread going back to Denver, I was hoping to shake it off in between shots and selfies, but I couldn't stop myself from looking at my phone, hoping to see a text.

I had been here before. When I arrived in Santa Barbara, I had promised myself I would heal. I would move on. I spent hours talking with Emily about him, how I was so hurt, but also how I didn't know how to move forward. Each visit to the beach, or moment of intoxication, I thought about reaching out. I didn't. I had been strong and had stood my ground, not bending to the courage one gets after a few drinks. Six months in Santa Barbara, and I had made major progress, but I wasn't done. He had no idea I was still thinking about him, and I wanted it that way. I was going to win this game. I will not look weak or silly. I won't be roped into thinking something was left when he hadn't reached out at all. I will not text him!

Now it had been an entire year, more than 365 days. I wasn't checking my texts nearly as much, and was now able to get through an entire yoga class without crying—all good signs! I was moving on!

I reactivated, but also quickly deleted, my Tinder app a handful of times. Online dating was weird for me. I was always overthinking it and felt too responsible for other people's feelings. Unnecessarily answering every message sent my way and awkwardly letting them down with, "It's not you. It's me," all before being asked out. I have never been a good pen pal anyway—too much chitter chatter and not enough action. I didn't like the idea of being labeled a Tinder-date, and leaned on old flames and past possibilities that were all more readily available. That was my comfort zone. I didn't want to start over with a stranger.

I had just a tiny cirrus cloud over me. It had nearly dissipated, but it was definitely still there. He was still there in my mind. We had conveniently seen one another for the first time since our break-up a year prior, right before I left for Mississippi. It was a fabulous night, one of those nights where everything seemed to go right back to the way it was. I was taken back in time, laughing and kissing, touching. Naturally, I stayed the night, which is exactly how it started. What else would you expect? Then I left without saying much. I hoped he would talk to me, but he never did, which drove me to write this crazy, impulsive, passionate, and intense email that would probably scare him off for good.

I wondered to myself if this was just a one and done, just a moment of weakness. I had been known for being a repeat offender in the past, continuing to go back to the toxic relationship I had in high school that lasted on and off throughout college. When I finally met Jay, I changed my ways and never felt the urge to run back to my first love. He was it, and I knew that, but did he?

I was heading back to Denver, starting a new chapter, moving out of my parents' house again and finally into my own apartment; yet this cloud was still over me and I had to know—was it real? Was this guy actually someone I needed to focus on?

I just simply wasn't dating material, a wanderer, floating around the country, getting paid under the table. I wasn't an adult. I was "just a nanny" who was trying to get a job as an illegitimate teacher. Who would want to date someone like me? Nothing about my situation screamed stability or commitment; I wouldn't even want to date me.

Therein lies the problem. I wasn't being the person I wanted to date. I loved this man because of his stability, his normalcy, and the safety that surrounded him. He had a normal childhood, parents who were still together, and compared to my experience growing up, I didn't feel good enough, but I knew what I had seen in the families I had been working for, my desire for normalcy, for regularity, predictability, and routine was something I wanted so badly now more than ever.

It wasn't until this moment that I realized how much of my history with my father was fueling my current decision-making. Often feeling unaccepted by my dad, combined with the rejection from jobs, schools, and men, I was in the habit of jumping from one thing to the next. Pulling the ripcord to immediately get away was my mechanism for survival. Alcoholism runs in my family, and I had pinpointed some of the same behaviors I saw in my dad in myself during college, but reluctantly pushed the signs away. It wasn't until my dad became sober four years later, in the midst of writing this book, that I am able to see my actions as symptoms coming from a familiar vein.

Some people say, "When you know, you know," referring to the person they are to spend forever with. I guess you can say that I knew but trust me, everyone thought I was crazy, for this was not a story of instant gratification. I moved across the country, twice, and in separate directions to escape my feelings, and it took about two years for us to come back around to each other, to grow a little, and finally move in together when I was 27 years old.

Before him, I had been stuck in this self-loathing pattern— led astray by my ex-boyfriends, time after time getting hurt but somehow expecting a different result, thinking that what they gave me was love, when really it was only attention given for convenience. I allowed it to happen for more years than I want to admit. Starting when I was 14 years old and lasting well into my mid-twenties, these types of guys were no good for me, and I knew it.

At 19, I walked into a tattoo parlor in Salt Lake City. I guess this is a habit of mine. In opposition to how I had been treated, I asked to get *Corinthians 13:4* tattooed on my back. "Love is patient, love is kind." It was located horizontally across the middle of my back where, in case I needed to hide the ink from my father, my bathing suit would hopefully cover the small font. Rebellion in tiny letters; I have always been a secret rule breaker. We loved shoplifting in high school because we could get away with it and smoking pot in the church parking lot because, well, white privilege explains most of it.

After I branded myself with the Bible's definition of love, my brain shifted. I could no longer punish myself with repeating my past mistakes. The minute I met Jay, I knew I would have an amazing future with him. At this time in my life, I had reached a point when I knew that it would take courage to get what I wanted. It would take vulnerability and it would take some grit. I was up for it and charging straight into the fight.

"Love is patient, it's kind, it doesn't envy, doesn't boast, isn't proud, isn't rude. Love always protects, always trusts, always hopes, and always perseveres" (1 Corinthians 13:4). This verse carried me through breaking my self-deprecating routine with my ex. It helped me understand why my mom never divorced my dad. It carried me through my dating dry spells, and when Jay and I finally reconnected, it carried me forward into what I now know is my future.

It leaves me dumbfounded to look back on this time and understand the significance of the pain and the struggle.

I blindly fought for what I wanted, and I am so glad I did. For going back to Denver was a toss-up. The result would be burn or growth, no in between.

CHAPTER TWELVE

Back to Denver

"Let me show you how it works," My dad said, sweating bullets, standing over the massive air conditioning unit he bought for me while I was away in Mississippi. The unit turned on with a rumble and started generating cool air into my tiny apartment. My lease had started a week or so before I was ready to come back, and for whatever reason, I gave my parents' permission to get my keys and check out the place for me; thus, in that time, they had checked all the fire alarms, locks, water pressure, and evaluated that it was too goddamn hot for their little 26-year-old daughter to stand. Believe me, Mississippi was hotter, but July in Denver can get warm, especially in a building designed in 1940 with brick walls, trapping heat like an oven.

"This fuckin' place," Dad said. "I mean it's cool, but I can't believe they can rob you guys blind, paying for a place without AC." By "you guys" he meant people my age, millennials. As my dad loves to point out extremely often, I am a millennial, and we live against the grain, pave our own path, take out too many loans, etc. He admitted he's dumbfounded by my "lifestyle," can't believe I move so much and change jobs more than I move. He has recently started calling me his "gypsy daughter." Though I don't recall gypsies having parents to mooch off, or parents of gypsies having a roof over their head. Not to mention, the term *gypsy* isn't too PC anymore. I rolled my eyes and attempted to help him secure the jury-rigged AC unit to the window screen that he cut a hole in, which will undoubtedly come out of my security deposit.

"Well it's a good thing I'm done teaching at that school," my mom said. Her petite stature and A-line mom-bob was bouncing all over the room, repositioning picture frames and opening all my cabinet doors.

"Mom, stop. Seriously, you're stressing me out. Just sit down," I told her.

She hopped up on the chair at my high-top table. I was so proud that I found that thing on Amazon—it fit perfectly in my kitchen, living room, and dining room corner.

"I can't believe I had to buy that AC unit for my classroom," Mom said. "It cost $300.00, and do you think Denver Public Schools paid me back? No, of course not." She was swinging her legs a foot above the ground. "They had to be crazy to think I was gonna let my seven-year-old babies sweat their little selves to death while I'm trying to teach reading. Ridiculous."

That's how underfunded some of the schools were in Denver. After the recession in 2008, my mom had a thousand interviews, trying to get back to work after taking the past seven years off. She had missed out on too many educational changes and completely missed when they covered how to teach in the digital age. While my sister and I were in elementary school learning how to play Oregon Trail and how to save data on a floppy disk, my mom was at home. She went back for a few years, but was primarily at home when I was in middle school.

After a stint of depression, a few separations from my dad, and make-ups with him too, she finally landed a job. It was across town, near the old Air Force base, which was now pretty run down, and primarily African-American.

The principal of the elementary school said he used to be a prison guard; he was horrible. My mom was a part-time reading teacher. She had no room that year, just a section of the end of the hall. She put up cute little curtains so her students would feel like they had some privacy. She worked her ass off.

She soon left and went to a teacher-led school on the west side of town. This time her students were primarily Latino and at least half were still learning English. My mom may have beautiful brown skin and dark jet-black hair, but she can't speak a lick of Spanish. My sister and I were mortified the last time we went to Tres Amigos Mexican Restaurant, and mom pronounced "pollo" [in Spanish, double l equals the Y sound] as "polo." She would teach second grade at that school for nearly four years, making money so I could go to college. I have never had enough words to share my gratitude to her. She bought that AC unit, and one more just like it for her students. One August and September, her classroom reached a high of 98 degrees. "Poor babies."

"Now that we have all this weed money though, I think they are going to put one of those swamp coolers in the classroom," mom said with her country drawl. All this time in Colorado and she still sounds like she is back in Arkansas, saying she lives in "Colorada," yes, with an 'A' on the end. Colorado had just passed the legalization of recreational marijuana, and the industry vowed to contribute its tax revenue directly to the public-school system. Colorado teachers are paid the second lowest in the country. They start out at a measly $39,000 a year but for me at the time that $39,000, might as well of been 100K.

I shooed them out after a while, lay flat on my Ikea bed that literally was in a bag an hour ago, and picked up my phone. All alone and what do I do? That's right. Think about Jay. I resisted the urge to text him and texted the few girlfriends I had left in Denver. I had a little less than two weeks until training would begin for my first teaching job ever. I was ready to blow off some steam, I spent the following 14 days making my French press coffee, reactivating and deleting Tinder, going to the community yoga class down the street, and getting to know some of my new neighbors on the stoop outside our building—my attempt at being Sarah Jessica Parker, but with more craft beer and fewer cosmopolitans.

I felt tired. I felt exhausted. I had been through so many moves, so many moments of disappointment, saying goodbye to people, leaving families I nannied for, kids I cared about, trying to convince my parents of the next plan that would work much better. I started school again, isn't that enough? I had finally landed a job that I knew would pay me enough to live on my own, take on some of my bills, and become more financially independent. I am 26 years old for God's sake! I'm not even covered by Obamacare anymore! I didn't have a dime in my savings account, had thankfully paid off my first credit card, but was probably running on a pathetic $200.00 balance in my checking, give or take $50.00.

I had had so many failed attempts at getting somewhere—a seasonal job here, part-time job there, paying for insurance out of pocket, and resorting to becoming a nanny to make just enough money while trying to "figure out my life."

I thought, was it just me?

The answer was no. It wasn't just me.

Every person I met in their early twenties felt a similar sense of despair. Why was it that our lives hadn't cracked up to what they were meant to be? Did our parents feed us lies as kids, telling us we could be whatever we want if we go to college? Then we graduate and we certainly cannot be whatever we want. Maybe it's the entitlement that millennials supposedly feel, that we all should get a trophy just for showing up? Why shouldn't we feel entitled? We just spent four to five years on our parents' dime and taking out federal loans, looking at a future of debt, working our asses off to be unemployed?

Most of us were wishing to make an impact on the world, to work to better the human race, the environment, and save the polar bears. At the very least, we wanted to have jobs where we can be slightly creative, innovative, and cool. Rather, we find ourselves working eight-hour days in an office, staring at a screen doing remedial tasks that a monkey could do, or better yet, a computer.

On another side of despair, why is it that I could name 15 women who had nanny passes to the Denver Zoo? What the hell was going on here?

While it had been explained to me how high the unemployment rate was, that more graduates were moving back in with their parents, and rent prices were rising, I couldn't help but take all of this very personally. I couldn't help feeling incapable, like I had no skills, nothing to offer, like I wasn't employable at all. It was crazy that I pulled off this teacher interview and actually got the job. The whole thing just felt suspicious, like this was almost too good to be true.

Come to find out, it was.

Fast forward three months and 21 days, and I was packing up my classroom. I had quit. Didn't even make it to Thanksgiving break.

Writing a goodbye note to my favorite student on a special postcard I had been saving from Santa Barbara, I sealed it and left it in her student mailbox. I had been let down once more. Disappointed and broken beyond belief, someone had dropped the ball, and it wasn't me. I totally got screwed.

The charter school movement in Colorado took off in the early 2000s when teachers and educational professionals were fed up with the local state government telling them how to run their schools, the way they must spend their money, how the teachers must teach, packing on more and more statewide tests, and confining their craft to a point where they had no autonomy. I like to compare charter schools to the Native-American Indian reservations. Indian reservations are sovereign nations ruled by themselves under the guise of the greater United States government. They have complete autonomy over how they spend their money, such as on casinos, but they still receive government funding, go by their own rule of law, and every once in a while, the U.S. government comes in to assist.

Charters have complete power over what they decide to do with their school with the benefit of the government funding as well. As we know now, we don't have a one-size-fits-all solution to all the inequities and issues we have with our education system here in the United States. Charter schools are just one solution. The types of charters are as numerous as breeds of dogs, and this one in particular was a full-bred, so perfectly crafted that it could be replicated over and over again without fail, but due to its lack in biodiversity, it's bound to not last for too long.

This school was a part of a larger charter school network, like a mini district within the larger Denver Public School District. All their schools were strategically located in some of the worst neighborhoods in Denver, where crime was high and schools were closing. They claimed to be the solution to turning around impoverished schools and neighborhoods, and they had money coming from more than the state. Sounds inspiring, right? That's exactly why I wanted to work for this school in the first place.

When public schools close, students are failing to a point where the state can't afford to keep the schools running. Schools close and it causes the already struggling neighborhoods to struggle even more. Parents with few resources have to find alternative transportation to get their kids to a school further away. Property values go down in the area, and families are forced to move. It's a trickle-down effect that can have a negative impact for decades.

Then, along comes this charter network that I will call ACHIEVE. They prevented the school from closing its doors and the kids got to stay where they'd been. No harm, no foul—a solution to the problem.

In the education world, educational philosophy is everything. Some lean towards hippy, holistic methods like Montessori, and others more towards scientific and standardized education, but most people don't get to pick the kind of education their kid gets at their local public school. What you get is what you get. If you have the privilege to choose, it's going to cost you.

As for these neighborhoods, they don't get to choose, so when a charter school swoops in to save the day, you follow suit and consider it a win. Kids who were failing are now being challenged, their grades are going up, and they can look you in the eye and tell you what college they want to go to, but this puzzle has another side. How is it that schools can get disengaged students and their parents reengaged in their school? The answer is the same for how 18-year-olds become prepared to follow an army sergeant and go to war—submission.

In a militaristic fashion, students' autonomy over themselves disappeared. They were forced to wear uniforms, unable to express their individual selves with their appearance. At 13 years old, appearance might just be the only way they know how to express themselves. Beside Snapchat filters, what else can a teenager do to explore their identity? Without wearing a Hurley hoodie and JNCO jeans at 13, I don't know who I'd be!

The school's theory is that eliminating the distraction leaves more space for kids to focus on their schoolwork. They may be right, or maybe it just crushes their souls.

Passing periods are also eliminated. Students are filed into the hallways one by one in complete silence to be escorted like prisoners from one room to another. This dance is a strange thing to witness, as nearly all of the staff are mid-twenties white adults, and all the kids span a range of brown, tan, and gold. As a teacher, I was instructed on every move I made and every word I spoke, practicing particular sentences we would repeat to students to require their submission. I even learned how and where in the room to stand to command the most attention and see the entire room. A demerit system was in place, and as the sergeant, it was my duty to look for wrongdoers and hand those demerits out like candy. I would often get in trouble for recording too few demerits. Lunch was supervised by the teachers (no rest for the weary), and kids sat in assigned seats, raising their hand to ask for permission just to go to the waste basket. I am not describing a correctional facility or a military boot camp. I am describing the neighborhood school that was the only one available.

My sensitive-Sally self could not handle the discipline. I wanted to hug the kids, listen to their worries, give them space to express themselves, and freedom in my classroom to be teenagers. Within the first month we lost two teachers. That number grew to three the following month. I, like many teachers who teach for Colorado charter schools, did not have a teaching license under the Colorado Department of Education. It would cost me another year and $3,000.00 to get it. Charters have been able to hire unlicensed teachers because they are sovereign nations, merely requiring a teacher to be "highly qualified." To prove I was highly qualified to teach, I took a state-mandated test to show I knew enough about the topic I planned to teach.

This is the catch. Audrey and standardized tests do not mix. I picked social science degrees for a reason, so I didn't have to take standardized tests. Ask me to write a paper and I'll prove that I walked on the moon. Sit me in a cold room in front of a computer with a page of scratch paper and a #2 pencil, and expect me to do no better than a monkey. Believe me, I tried. I studied on Saturdays in between crying fits of exhaustion and worry. After taking the test for the third time, having spent more than $450.00, I was still one measly point away. They had reduced my salary to substitute pay, which was $98.00 a day with the same course load and responsibilities.

I became the fourth teacher to quit that semester. I was crushed.

I was ugly crying in my car at 7:00 p.m., having just found the last parking space on my block, so tired I could hardly muster up the strength to grab all my bags and walk up two floors to my apartment. "I don't want to leave my kids. They are finally starting to like me. Leslie doesn't even call me a bitch anymore," I said to my mom on the phone. "They witness people leaving them all the time. I don't want to be someone who leaves them!" I was sobbing at this point, my mom trying to offer me any kind of comfort she could.

"It's not even worth it," mom said. "You have to quit. It's okay it didn't work out. Something else will!" The last thing she wanted was for me to suffer at a school like she did. Like many public-school teachers, you try to teach your students, but spend most of the time trying to deal with behavior problems that arise when one parent is in jail and the other works three jobs. With little guidance or supervision at home, kids come to school and are hungry, tired, and lost. It becomes nearly impossible to require their focus on something like multiplication tables.

The kids were pushing back on the tight rules and constraining environment. I wasn't being paid enough to pay my rent that month because I had spent my last paycheck on taking the goddamn test. I was done.

Charter schools like this one recruit recent college graduates promising a "Freedom Writers" or "Stand and Deliver" experience—empowering poor city kids to strive for the top and go to college because their white teacher plays instrumental hip hop during independent reading time. Teachers enlist with the intention to help and "save" the students from their impoverished situations full of substance abuse and teen pregnancy. Dropout rates are alarmingly high in Denver and the publicly funded school system, even with all the "weed" money, just isn't cutting it.

At the end of the day, with all my experience taking care of babies, wiping little butts, doing laundry, and offering daily laughs and hugs to moms, I wasn't really made out for being called a bitch in front of an entire class and dealing with some of the issues my students faced daily. I was too weak to make it through. That's okay.

I'm not afraid to say it. I decided that paying my rent with my student loans and finishing the degree that I was second guessing was the only sure thing I had going. I was determined to pass that test, even if it would be another $180.00 down the drain. Though my loans could cover my rent, it couldn't cover everything else. I picked up a housesitting gig, walked a few dogs, and helped a former colleague plan a Martin Luther King Day fundraiser in January. I applied for positions here and there, going around this tree for the hundredth time. I wasn't too enthusiastic. A few interviews and rejections later, I knew where I had to go. I reluctantly resorted to nannying. I was reaching 27, and I seemed to be exactly where I was before. I was watching daytime television in someone's living room with my shoes on, waiting for a baby to wake up from its nap.

PART III

CHAPTER THIRTEEN

The Business of Nannying

I met the coolest girl during my brief stint at ACHIEVE. She had a full sleeve of tattoos, black-rimmed glasses, and lived in the pre-gentrified neighborhood close to school. Well, maybe her existence now makes it gentrified, actually. She said, "I just moved here from Indiana with my boyfriend. He works for a little coffee start up. I'm the art teacher." She introduced herself to me, so relaxed and put together.

We immediately became work buddies, sitting next to one another at training by choice but also by force. The English and Art departments were clumped together for content meetings.

We weren't complaining.

Training was a month long. Mary was a trained teacher and had been teaching for four years already. Though she had a license, it was from Indiana and therefore would take a few months to be recognized by the State of Colorado. She needed a job as soon as possible, so she figured a charter couldn't be that bad. Like me, she interviewed and was offered the job on the spot. That should have been our first sign of trouble.

My car broke down the first day of training and my new teacher-friend drove me home that day. Was that an omen that this job would also break me down? Yes, I am sure of this, as the rest of this story doesn't have a happy ending for either of us.

We later bonded over a shared yoga class. Sharing a yoga class with a new friend was truly the ultimate test of measuring whether I could be work-friends or friend-friends with this girl. By agreeing to said yoga class, I knew this chick was my kind of gal pal. We were willing to see each other in skin-tight stretch pants and not be embarrassed by our cellulite showing through as we forward-folded together. That is immediate acceptance of oneself and of others in this strange world where most, if not all, women suffer from some kind of body image issues. Going to yoga with a new friend is completely off the table sometimes if you're over a size 10. Mary and I were about size 10, if you even agree with the numerical scale of measuring a woman's body, so the common ground thankfully enabled us busty blondes to enjoy the first of many times downward-dogging and frog-posing in unison.

We finished training together over that month, she bestowing her years of teacher knowledge on me as we prepared for the semester to begin. School began, and we caught each other's looks of dismay and fright in the hallway. She shared with me what it was like to teach at a "normal" school, as she called it.

She sarcastically remarked, "You know, where you can let the kids chit chat with each other while they're drawing in art class." Mary was the second teacher to quit in the first two months. Witnessing the battle she was fighting with herself was like looking in a mirror. I was also struggling with my job, wanting to quit every day.

It was a horrible experience for everyone, and she was heartbroken. In the meantime, I attempted my best to hang onto my sanity, and she encouraged me all along, being the voice of reason. She needed to get out of there and without time to have a back-up plan, I suggested what seemed to help me in my times of need—nannying.

I said, "Just get on Care.com. You're a teacher for crying out loud, you'll get a job in a heartbeat." Within a few weeks, Mary had a job and began nannying for a cute little family with tow-head blonde toddlers. Making money under the table isn't exactly what it's cracked up to be when you're a law-abiding citizen like Mary. She often was worried about insurance, and come April, what would happen if she didn't file taxes? I'm not sure what she did in the end, but two years later, she's still nannying, so take that for what it's worth.

After a breakup with her boyfriend in Colorado, Mary moved down the street from me in Capital Hill for the next six months. Soon thereafter, nannying enabled her to move to one of her bucket-list places, Portland, Oregon. Off chasing bearded men and artistic ventures, Mary is now on to her second family in Portland, considering another move if she can find a family to work for.

I remember telling her, "Welcome to the babysitters club!" We were cheersing our craft beers at our favorite dive bar where we'd meet weekly for the next year or so. It was halfway between our sketchy neighborhoods, next to a Whole Foods and adjacent to a little homeless camp, or rather, homeless gathering, that was a handful of people who camped out nightly. What a dichotomy this place was.

At that point, I had no idea Mary would renew her hypothetical "babysitters club" membership for the following three years. Leaving her teaching years behind her for now, she entered her thirties that year, and like many of us, was using nannying to cope with unemployment, high rent prices, and in her case, it actually got her out of Colorado to where she wanted to be.

I always thought that I should start charging membership fees to this hypothetical babysitters' club. It's not even hypothetical at this point—there are my Midwestern girls, my East Coast girls, my Southern girls and of course my Southwest girls.

Nannies in the Midwest include:

Janie from Wisconsin, a graduate student in Psychology, 27 years old. Mary from Indiana and a licensed teacher of five years, with a bachelor's degree in art education, 29 years old. Katherine from Iowa with a bachelor's degree in social work and a social worker for four years, 28 years old.

Nannies on the East Coast include:

Ellie from Pennsylvania with a bachelor's degree in environmental science, 24 years old. Harper from New Jersey has a bachelor's degree in environmental science, 24 years old. Naomi from Pennsylvania has a bachelor's degree in Biochemistry and is 25 years old.

Nannies in the Southern United States include:

Mildred from North Carolina, with a bachelor's degree in meteorology, 24 years old. Kara from Oklahoma has a bachelor's degree in marketing and graphic design, 23 years old.

In the Southwest, nannies include:

Misty, who has a master's degree in education, 24 years old. Hayley, who is a licensed massage therapist, 25 years old. Denise from New Mexico has a bachelor's degree in education, 26 years old.

Colorado nannies include:

Lana with a master's degree in international development, 23 years old. Brandie with a bachelor's and master's degree in education, 32 years old. Nicky with a PhD in psychology, 26 years old. Janet with a bachelor's degree in sports medicine, 25 years old. Allie with a bachelor's degree in communications, 28 years old. Allie's mom nannied her entire career, and is 62 years old.

It is the start of 2016 and all these women—educated women—were nannying! Sure, it was a personal choice. I am sure that they could find a job somewhere else, but many women were in the midst of furthering their education, getting their master's or

Ph.D. degrees, unable to make enough cash with a typical $12.00 per-hour-wage at a retail store or coffee shop, so nannying was the bee's knees. Some of my teacher and social worker friends actually make more nannying full-time than they ever had with the Department of Education or Human and Social Services. A quarter of them used nannying to move to a place they have always wanted to go, including myself, or to get away from the place they currently were, also including myself. All these women are educated, white, and middle class, from supportive families that probably envisioned their daughters using their many degrees, but who wants to be an administrative assistant when you can go to the pool in the summer and museum in the winter?

This description of women is strikingly different from past generations of nannies, and some areas that are stuck in the past as well. It was like I was witnessing a cultural phenomenon of some kind. In Mississippi, the nanny career trajectory was mainly low-income women of color, mostly African-American. In Texas and California, tons of families have nannies from Central and Latin America, and many are first generation immigrants and largely low-income. If I thought my neighborhood was a dichotomy, this really is. What other career or job can claim to have this kind of diversity and variation?

Sure, I've heard of a Manny before, like a man_nanny, but that's pretty rare. We are white, educated women displacing women of color from the jobs in areas millennials are flocking to. In 2016, the top place millennials were moving was Denver. "Transplants galore," my other native Coloradan friends would joke.

Realizing my missed opportunity to capitalize on the nannying market, plenty of businesses were already revolving around pairing families with nannies, such as Care.com, mommyandme.com, and plenty of local nanny agencies. I was now at a point where I needed to find myself my next nanny gig. Care.com was a pain in the ass to navigate, so using a real human being to help me find the next family seemed very attractive.

Mary had met with someone she found who ran her own nanny placement agency in Denver, called The Nanny Shop—what a weird concept. I envisioned framed pictures of young beautiful nannies with psychology, art, and education degrees from well-known universities hanging on the walls of a high-end boutique in the old money Bonnie Brae Denver neighborhood. Women with fur coats filter around the room with their pensive hand-to-chin poses, studying the pictures and reading the descriptions as if they were in an art gallery. Meanwhile, their kids are crawling around the floor in their Louis Vuitton pampers, and the mother tries to sense whether the nanny could be someone she would have a glass of wine with, but who would also act as the subordinate when power plays present themselves.

"They can't be too pretty," the ladies said. "We don't want our husbands to get any ideas."

"They can't be too young. I need someone I can talk to but also someone who's responsible enough to show up to work on time."

"They can't be too old. Johnny is super rambunctious and he needs someone who can keep up."

"I want them to speak Spanish, but they really need to know English as well. I would love if my kids could be bilingual. That is super employable nowadays."

"Well, they definitely need their own car and have room for the car seats. My husband and I are using our own cars and don't have an extra one. We'll give her $50.00 a month for gas. That's no big deal."

Mary almost scored a job working for an NBA player, but they wanted someone to live with them full-time. Since she was newly single, that was off the table. You can't bring a guy back from a Tinder date to your place of work to hook up—that's just weird. She settled for working 35 hours a week with a quaint family of four in the gentrified, new-money neighborhood called the Highlands.

Both parents managed multiple restaurants in Denver, so her schedule would vary, sometimes going super late into the night, but the money was worth it, and so were the kids. Parker and Ranger, 6- and 3-year -olds, respectively, became super close to Mary. The closer they got, the harder it became for Mary to decide when or if she was going to move to Portland like she had wanted to do for years. She eventually left. The kids were sad, but they had a new nanny the next week. The cycle goes on.

I played with the idea of being Mary's fill-in. I was currently on the third family in four months. Being thrown around like a rag doll from one family to the next, I was these families' emergency plan. I figured that they were my emergency plan as well.

CHAPTER FOURTEEN

The Woman's Predicament

They couldn't find a better nanny than me. I was like Mary Poppins at this point, with all my experience teaching, and working in schools. I even went to Disneyland with a kid who hardly spoke English. I started singing supercalifragilisticexpialidocious to myself as I drove to my next nanny interview, my brain going on a tangent wondering why Mary Poppins forced the kids to drink cough syrup even though they weren't sick, and remembering that cute little advertisement the kids came up with to look for their "perfect nanny." If only that was the way it worked, and I could arrive at all jobs by umbrella instead of my road bike.

I planned to meet Jessa at 1:30 p.m. at the Starbucks on Second Avenue in Cherry Creek. She was the owner of the Nanny Shop. I wasn't sure what I was going to get myself into, whether she would place me with ritzy millionaires or just regular people like Mary's family.

In my situation, I was still holding out for a job, like a real job, but it was getting down to the wire and I was still waiting for interviews and whatnot. I figured I could pass the time nannying for a family, and use all the down time I would have to apply to jobs and do my school work.

I walked into Starbucks looking around blankly at some of the people sitting at the scattered tables. I told Jessa that I would be wearing a green blouse, and soon enough a woman was walking up to me. She was very pregnant, beach-ball-under-the-shirt pregnant. The irony of meeting her, the woman who finds nannies, likely needing a nanny herself pretty soon, was slightly amusing to me. Then again, maybe she wouldn't need a nanny, maybe she has the best of all worlds. She can work, have coffees with potential nannies and families, and work from home, enabling her to take care of her own baby while also making a living. She's a genius! She's cracked the code!

Maybe, though, she can't afford a nanny because she gets such little pay from families if she finds them a nanny, but not until she successfully places one. I inquired about all of these details, acting as if I was interested in starting my own agency. She happily told me how it works, but also shared that it was difficult to pin down a "good one," as she put it.

She described the typical nanny as a young girl who would temporarily work with a family until something better came along. She seemed a bit annoyed by this inconvenient truth, as she was constantly trying to find replacements for the nannies she placed with families only months before.

I was one of those "young girls," but getting older by the second and figured I would cut to the chase. I needed a temporary gig, something for the next few months.

"I don't want to sign my life away because I'll probably get a job soon," I told her. "I would ideally nanny for a family that doesn't need someone permanently, just for the time being."

She was surprised by my honesty. Usually people pretend that they intend to help raise kids for the next few years, but end up branching off and scoring a spot on the Bachelor or going to graduate school, leaving the family before their first-year mark. Jessa described the rarity of someone my age with experience with infants and told me she has plenty of families looking for interim-nannies, which would fit well with my commitment issues.

The interim-nanny is hired for an undefined amount of time. It could be a number of weeks or months that fall between maternity leave ending and their child's name making it to the top of their chosen daycare or preschool. Moms all over Denver were freaking out, trying to find a nanny before they had to go back to work.

"Sure," I nodded along. "Sign me up." It sounded like a strange need that I could fill—a reciprocal situation. I need a job for a little bit, and they needed a nanny for a little bit. Both parties win, right?

Jessa had a family in mind. She said they had a 3-month-old named Callie, and the nanny she had placed with them a few months prior was moving away, but they still hadn't heard back from the preschool they were hoping to get the baby into. The mother was frantically looking for help starting as soon as possible, as she was going back to work in a week and suddenly had no one to watch over her precious, first-born child. I happily stepped in and showed up the following week for my first full eight-hour day with baby Callie.

This was a cute little family of three, transplants from Chicago. Sam (Samantha) and Will had met on Match.com in their early thirties. They had pictures of their wedding in Mexico all over the house, and it looks like they got a bit sunburned before tying the knot—a pretty classic white-shirts-and-no-shoes beach wedding. He was a CrossFit enthusiast, often coming home from work to chug a quick protein drink and head to the gym. The mom left an hour or so after I got there each morning and was in sales for dermatology pharmaceuticals, often driving around in a suit and high heels, sometimes just to deliver coffee and pastries to clients she was trying to butter up. She had just started a new position. Excited to get back to work, she shared with me a few of her worries during this transitional time in her life.

Though we hardly knew one another, nothing is more personal than taking care of another woman's baby. This human, the baby, was literally inside this other person, the mother, and now it is my job to make sure both these humans stay fed, clothed, and taken care of, so to speak. It's normal to talk about the baby's poop color and how many times she burped, but what happens between those conversations are personal talks about their marriage, their feelings, hopes, worries, and grievances. Remembering Jenn's woes and worries, I was able to resonate with some of Sam's. Going back to work isn't easy for any mom. With the biological pull to be close to your baby, your brain can barely think about anything else, and when trying to transition back to working-mom mode, often it feels straining and difficult to focus. Sam was not only feeling all of this, but she was also starting a brand-new job. Some of the people she worked with made comments about how much she had missed while she was "off." She was so angry that people kept calling it her time "off." Once she said, "Time off, more like, time on. Time on the toilet, time on the hospital bed, time on at 3 a.m., time on at 4 a.m.!"

One particular day, Sam came home earlier than usual and she asked me to stay later. She told me that she'd be upstairs for a while but I could still leave at 5:30 p.m. like normal. I didn't think twice about it, and waited for Callie to get up from her nap to go on our afternoon walk around the block.

When we got back to the house, Sam had poured herself some wine and was sitting on the couch downstairs. We came in, the massive bulldog they had drooling and charging the door, followed by their little Chihuahua yip yapping; what an odd couple.

Sam looked like she had been crying, and impulsively I said, "Oh no, what's wrong?! Is everything ok?"

Why can't I just ignore things? What if she doesn't want to talk about it? Do you even want to talk about it, Audrey? Good going, I regretted to myself.

"Well, I got fucking fired today, dude!" Sam explained, almost splashing her wine out of her glass.

She didn't meet some kind of numbers at work and they let her go with no notice at all. She was confused. Her company expected her to meet a quota that she simply couldn't meet because she had been on maternity leave. She felt like her maternity leave counted against her, and it seems it definitely did! Her quota was the same as her teammates, yet she only had half the time to accomplish it.

In the sales world of meeting quotas and working off commission, when would be a good time to have a baby? Pretty much never. In a male-dominated field, sales industries may offer maternity leave, but do they plan accordingly so the numbers don't bite the woman in the ass later? In Sam's case: nope.

In shock, I took Callie out of her stroller and we sat down next to Sam, listening to her story and her worries about paying for this expensive preschool and her husband's boat. I wondered in the back of my head how this would also affect my life. If Sam doesn't have to work then what does she need me for?

My sympathy quickly turned into selfish worry. What will I do about rent this month? I had just had my second interview with a nonprofit youth development organization for a real full-time job with benefits. I felt super confident about the interview, and I even knew someone who helped me get my resume to the hiring committee. I was currently working at an elementary school on the days I wasn't with Callie, and was starting to think I couldn't possibly risk teaching for another charter that might blow up in my face later on.

I knew at this point that I had no control over what was happening around me. That rang true more than ever in this moment. Now that Sam had lost her job, I had two weeks on the clock to muscle up a new plan, hopefully get a job offer, or hope at the least that Jessa could find me a new family. I rolled my eyes. Here we go again!

I pulled out of their driveway on my last day with Callie, trying not to feel completely and utterly defeated. I had finally heard back from the organization, where I interviewed, and they decided to hire internally. Of course.

As I was driving back to my little studio, all I wanted was to have a drink and a long drag from an American Spirit cigarette. Taking deep breaths, filling my lungs with air, following my yoga teachers' instructions, I made my way back to my apartment in one piece. Laughing to myself as I parallel parked behind someone's bumper sticker that read, "Keep Calm and Carry On," I sat in my car and cried for a little while. I didn't call my mom this time. I just cried to myself, praying that I would be able to follow the bumper sticker's advice.

Growing Pains—Transitional woes

I found myself asking, Why me? Why had things been so hard for me? My inability to fit this mold that my parents laid out was starting to catch up with me. At first, I really felt that beating my own drum and leading my own path would leave me feeling triumphant and excited. I felt like that for a while, like I was being led somewhere, to my truth, to my purpose. I certainly had moments of purpose when helping Jenn with Ava, or saving the day with little Gio as his emergency caregiver, but I wanted a path towards a career—a real job.

I wanted to prove to my parents and everyone else that I could be successful. Much of our adult lives are spent seeking approval. We have that one person in our lives that we hope one day to wow.

For me, it was my father. In his eyes, I was unstable, flighty, and following the pursuit of happiness. In other words, I was listening to the big government, liberal media too much. Me and all the other millennials are all lost, entitled, and over educated about conspiracy theories and only want to do "feel good" jobs, as he put it.

I was lost, and I was exhausted, just as my dad told me I would be.

My love for teaching, working with kids, and helping young people find their way seemed to have a limit. I could never make enough to pay my rent on my own, and I obviously couldn't teach full time, especially not after this past experience. I thought about my next move. I knew that I had to pursue my teaching license in Colorado, but it wasn't as easy as one would think. A licensure is the only route to getting a salaried position with benefits and insurance as a teacher. The last thing I wanted was to get screwed over by another charter school, so this was really my only option as long as the nonprofit gatekeepers keep turning me away.

My student loans from this master's degree will be sky-high when I am finished. While exploring my options, I found that my online master's program offered only one licensure option: to do an online licensure program in Florida— Florida? After taking a number of tests in Florida, assuming I passed them, which wasn't very likely with my track record, I would come back to Colorado, take another test, and in the end, I would spend upward of $3,500.00.

How does any of that make sense?

Let's add this up:

Master's Degree equals about $38,000.

Teaching Licensure program equals about $2,000.

Teacher tests equal $160 to $180 X 4, totaling $640 to $720.

About $40,000 in debt to get paid $45,609.96 to teach for Denver Public Schools equals priceless.

	Years	BA	BA/30	BA/60	MA	MA/30	MA/60	Doctorate
Denver Public Schools ProComp Salary Setting - 2017 - 2018 Degrees/Credits Earned PRIOR Transferring or Joining DPS								
Years of Teaching Experience PRIOR to Transferring or Joining DPS (Equivalent Step on Table)	0 (Step 1)	41,689.08	41,985.20	42,278.33	45,609.96	45,609.96	46,432.83	49,261.52
	1 (Step 2)	41,991.15	42,370.59	42,754.49	45,996.84	45,996.84	48,600.84	51,557.50
	2 (Step 3)	42,104.24	42,633.96	44,397.24	46,260.22	47,453.60	50,520.36	53,612.43
	3 (Step 4)	42,311.07	42,857.16	46,002.80	46,483.42	49,206.46	52,408.64	55,624.20
	4 (Step 5)	42,681.58	44,577.29	47,898.51	48,203.55	51,218.24	54,558.80	57,917.21
	5 (Step 6)	42,930.08	46,410.51	49,876.06	50,036.76	53,323.76	56,801.21	60,320.33
	6 (Step 7)	44,681.45	48,321.10	51,910.16	51,945.87	55,551.29	59,144.81	62,851.42
	7 (Step 8)	46,505.74	50,267.40	54,048.41	54,048.41	57,848.76	61,610.43	65,488.16
	8 (Step 9)	48,392.52	52,366.97	56,295.29	56,295.29	60,251.88	64,244.19	68,242.44
	9 (Step 10)	50,389.42	54,529.04	58,661.21	58,661.21	62,797.85	66,918.12	71,120.24
	10 (Step 11)	52,456.25	56,755.08	61,082.19	61,082.19	65,376.56	69,731.93	74,130.46

Note: Up to 10 years of relevant full-time work experience within the past 15 years counts as a step on the salary schedule. Therefore, step 11 is the highest starting point for teachers in their first year at DPS.

*Annual salary is based on a 1488 hour (186 day) schedule. Annual salary will be adjusted based on the hourly rate and work year and prorated based on FTE.

It's not worth it, I thought to myself. I can't even consider this route. I'll be paying my loans until my kids are in college! Then I'll be taking out loans to pay my loans!

It's starting to make sense why my Dad doesn't believe in student loans. Maybe his conservative ass is right for once. It may just as well be a big government scam. I hate it when he's right.

Colorado is thirty third out of 50 states in the country for teacher salaries, paying teachers an average of $49,000 a year, depending on the district. It sounded like a lose-lose and exactly why my mom always discouraged my interest in becoming a teacher. She knew from experience that no matter how much you love children, and are devoted to teaching low-income kids, the system breaks you down and eventually you cave or you become a bitter old lady. No wonder the teacher in Charlie Brown has no identity—she lost it a long time ago and is going to ride it out till retirement. "Whomp, whomp, whomp."

I circle back to what's real. What is actually paying my bills? Nannying.

Sure, it doesn't feel like a real job, but if a real job is one that pays, and a real job is one that people show up to every day, and everyone is doing a job that essentially fills a need of some kind, then I guess Nanny is a real job.

After finishing up with Callie, I was a few weeks away from finishing the spring semester at the elementary school where I was working as an aid a few afternoons during the week. Frantically formulating a summer plan, I tapped into all my resources. Though Jessa was still trying to find me my next family, she was about to have a baby herself, so I doubted I was at the top of her list of priorities. The school was trying to recruit me to teach fourth grade the next school year but with the politics in the educational system, and the bad taste that charter schools were leaving in my mouth, I was still feeling extremely hesitant to jump into teaching.

I decided I needed the summer to think it over. I needed some space, some time away from the fast pace of the classroom, and this past crazy school year. Scarred by my time at ACHIEVE, I needed some time to process my thoughts.

Remembering my previous summers nannying in Santa Barbara and then in Mississippi, a surge of nostalgia came over me. I felt so relaxed. I felt I was filling a need for the mothers and that felt so good—taking long walks, having those quiet moments with the babies, reading a book and stretching each summer day out for all it would lend us, wearing my stretch pants to work. Who else gets to say that, other than the Lulu Lemon sale associates and Pilates instructors?

I figured one more summer spent nannying wouldn't hurt, but I wondered if I could get away with one more tax-free summer off the books. How would the government know I was paid under the table? If I could find a family close by, I could spend my summer days biking back and forth to work, a short-term solution to the car problems I was having. I imagined taking long walks with a sleeping baby in a stroller, getting a little jog in and a nice sun tan. Nannying didn't sound like a bad way to spend the summer in Colorado.

I gave in.

I had just reached 27 and figured all the best rock and rollers survived till 27, so what's one more summer of shamelessly using my bachelor's degree to wipe butts and read Dr. Seuss books to other people's kids? I could go to whatever music show I wanted, and stay out as late as I wanted, because as long as the kid gets a nap at 9 a.m., then so do I.

I was hoping to score another interim-nanny job, and since Jessa was a little busy, I resorted to all the women I had come across in the past. Whether I had helped them for a random date night, walked their dog while they were at work, or fed their cat while they went to Hawaii, I texted everyone I knew. Learning about local Facebook groups and a new site called NextDoor, I asked some people I knew to post an advertisement for me titled: Nanny seeking summer work, experience with infants!

Though my ad sounded nothing like the Mary Poppins ad, I remembered the magical way in which Mary Poppins was sent to the family in the movie. After the children sing their advertisement song describing the attributes of their perfect nanny, the father is quick to dismiss them, rips up the paper, and throws it into the fireplace. As the children leave the room, the pieces of paper magically float up through the chimney and seemingly into the heavens.

The very next day, Mary Poppins shows up, via umbrella, I might remind you, and the family is suddenly blessed with the perfect woman to take care of the children for the remainder of the movie.

Though I am far from perfect, I will say I have a knack for nannying. I was able to find joy in each day with the children. Doing errands and chores wasn't the worst thing, and nothing felt better than greeting them when they got home and making parents feel confident that their child was in good hands. I loved holding babies and putting Band-Aids on boo-boos. A part of me that I didn't know existed came out each time I would care for another family. I loved being needed, and I loved knowing what it could be like to have a child myself or toy with the idea of one day being married. I knew what a good relationship looked like and what one that wasn't so good looked like. You never truly know if you can handle being a mom, but after witnessing the past moms tackle motherhood in a multitude of circumstances, I knew I could do it one day. This is biologically what we are made for. Though I support a woman's right to choose, and am a huge fan of birth control and plan B, we can populate the world after all, and that's pretty impressive.

The next three families I nannied for that summer might as well have sent a request into the universe because, indeed, they found their Mary Poppins. I didn't search for them. They found me through only a few degrees of separation. It was essentially like I floated down by umbrella.

I nannied for each family during some of their most vulnerable times as new parents. I know that each family had equally been sent to me and offered me gifts they never thought would be considered as such. I wouldn't go back and change it in the least. Though I declared this as my last summer of nannying ever, it was the one that tied it all together for me in the end, and I'd say it's worth sharing.

CHAPTER FIFTEEN

Summer of the Baby

Summer of 2016. It all started with a phone call.

Through an anonymous referral, I received a phone call one night from a woman named Kirsten. She was slightly erratic on the phone, and could hardly describe where she found my number or who gave it to her but she did make one thing clear, that she was in a hurry to find a nanny.

"Well, you see the daycare can't take her yet because they are full, and I have to go back to work, and I'm a little desperate," she said. I was in the bathroom at a restaurant when I answered her call. I figured it was better she heard flushing toilets than the Bob Marley this place was blaring.

I had heard this a dozen times and recognized her "new-mommy brain." Jenn explained that a new-mommy brain feels as if you are a zombie, your brain is mush, complemented by a blank stare when you interact with anyone except your child. She'd say it's as if every time the babies breast fed, they would eat some of your brain cells along with the breastmilk coming out of your body. Terrifying, if you think about it. She would often say her memory was useless. She felt increasingly disorganized, and often very frazzled. After hearing that, why would anyone trust a new mom? I drifted off into a demented scene where a mom is staring into space as their kid tumbles down the stairs. Lord, that lady needs a nanny! Snapping back from my dysfunctional thoughts, I agreed to meet

Kirsten and her baby the next day. She lived within biking distance from my apartment, so that was a good sign.

I returned to dinner with my friends, immediately excited that I had a lead and I could pay my friends back for the concert tickets they had spotted for me lately. It crossed my mind that this would be baby number four. At 27, I had more experience with infants than most moms gather in a lifetime. Though one could see this as honorable, special, a gift, nannying was my version of rebelling. I was making cash under the table and not using the degree my dad guilts me for getting every day.

Instead, I spent the summer caring for not one, not two, but three different babies. What followed was a season that I couldn't have dreamed into reality; what I like to call: Summer of the baby.

Double Duty

Kirsten had found another mom who was also looking for a nanny on NextDoor, which is like Facebook, but you only get to be friends with people in your neighborhood. Looking back, attempting to pilot a nanny share between two strangers was certainly tricky. I quickly morphed into what one might call a "Nanny-share consultant," sitting on a couch between two moms with my laptop on my lap. Creating a shared google calendar together, one mom was well-versed and the other was just being introduced to the glory of all that Google calendar means for collaborative childcare efforts. Merging two working mothers' schedules to create my daily work shifts took some creativity, prowess, and patience, as these schedules typically changed in an instant and often had a domino effect when things fell apart.

For three months we balanced this juggling act, Kirsten with her daughter Scarlet, and Brianna with her daughter Lola. Lola and Scarlet; sounds like I was working at a nursing home. With all the naps, the eating of soft foods, and the wiping of butts, I started considering a career in geriatric nursing... psych!

Kirsten and Scarlet

Scarlet Blue was perfect. She was round and pink, with soft blue eyes and a smiley grin. Gerber missed a huge marketing opportunity with this one. She's the baby every parent wishes they would end up adopting. Kirsten was 44 years old and had waited her entire life to have a child. She never married, but rather acquired five beautiful hens, two rescue dingo dogs, and owned her own artsy cottage in a middle-class (soon to be upper) area of East Parkview in Denver.

After seven tries, she almost gave up on her search for a child. She had been told many times that an adoption agency had a baby for her to pick up at a nearby hospital.

Six times in a row, the birth families changed their minds. That's worse than all of the 40 jobs I interviewed for and never got.

All the while, Kirsten had kept her eye on the prize, nicknaming her unborn baby "Blue." She finally got lucky with number seven. Kirsten arrived at the Denver hospital and finally met her true love. After so many times leaving empty-handed, Kirsten left the hospital with her hands full—very, very, full. She named her little girl Scarlet Blue, for her strawberry hair.

What might be worth telling is less about the babies and more about the incredible women and men raising them. I feel I was sent to each of them in their most delicate times as new parents, and they were equally sent to me in a time where I needed to be rooted to what was important in life—the real parts of humanity. I was witnessing the genuine connection that a mother and father have to a helpless little child—one of life's miracles.

I was a lost young woman, frustratingly running into roadblocks and financial barriers, unable to foresee my future. I felt rejection from what I needed and wanted, yet was conveniently placed in a position to learn from three successful women who inspired me to keep going. One holds a Ph.D. and taught at the urban college in Denver. The next was a teacher and single mom who had just adopted for her first time, and lastly, a local lawyer. These three showed strength, willpower, and incredible tenacity to do what many would think is impossible. Highly educated, giving birth and having a family would not hinder their careers. At the three-month marker ending their respective maternity leaves, each did their best to fight the attachment they had acquired with their children since they left the womb. Putting all their might into transitioning back into the professional world, it took an amount of courage that only a woman can understand. Pumping their breasts in closets, storing breastmilk in silly looking coolers that they would later have to take to their next meeting because they would get too warm if left in the car, they were furthering their careers, which had seemingly just begun, using their expensive degrees, determined to make an impact on the world. The only option they had was to find a caregiver. No one ever thinks about how hard it is to try to do it all, to be a mom and be a working woman. Society thinks that leaving your baby at three months should be fine, but at three months these kids are barely waking up to the world. They are so young that their little eyes are just starting to develop enough to recognize a stranger over their father. Meanwhile, the moms are expected to hand them over into the arms of a nanny as if it's no big deal.

As their interim nanny, I was essentially saving their asses. Waitlisted for the nearby preschool, avoiding exposing their newborns to the "frightening germs of Head Start programs" and overcrowded, government-approved childcare facilities, I was their best and most expensive bet. Paid more than a school teacher in Colorado, under the table, they were probably breaking even with paying me, all so the mom could return to work. It's this constant battle. Maybe financially it didn't make sense for some, but as a nanny I know how crazy you can feel, day in and day out feeling as if the world is going on without you, so I don't blame the mothers for getting back to work, for you see, the work we choose is often our life's purpose, or it finances our life's purpose.

The moms had stumbled upon a double stroller, apparently one of the nicest running strollers you can find. I certainly put some miles on that thing, walking twice a day in the dry Colorado heat. I ventured to the local library for mommy n' me story time and meeting up at the zoo with my other nanny friends in the babysitters club. Stuffing snacks in my pockets for later, I set my timer to go off every four hours so I remembered to give someone their bottle or put someone down for a much-needed nap. Their schedules and body clocks certainly was a science. I seemingly had this nanny thing-down!

Brianna and Lola

One afternoon, during the second nap of the day, I was exploring around the house. It's a strange experience getting used to a stranger's home. You learn where they keep their water glasses, their diuretics, what temperature to keep the thermostat turned to, and the little quirks of people's houses, pets, and personal lives.

"Make sure to hold the toilet handle down for at least three full seconds before letting it go."

"If the neighbors park their car in front of the driveway, please text me."

"If the chickens get out, call me ASAP."

"The mail person will come by at exactly 3:41 p.m. Just make sure you give the dogs a treat right then so they don't bark and wake Lola up."

Glancing at the photos on the fridge with admiration, wondering what my fridge with my family might look like one day, I saw a hand-written note signed, "Mom." The note was from Lola's grandmother, addressed to Lola's mom. The letter said something like this:

"Brianna,

I am so proud of you for putting Lola's health first, I know it has been hard to be off of your routine. Just know that you have done your very best, you have breastfed her as long as you personally are able, and it is okay to start taking your medicine again! You are not failing her. You are the best mom and you are making the right decision for you and your family.

Love,

Mom"

I sat down on the ground in the kitchen, and as one of the dogs ran to greet me, I wept for the many things that we never know we could go through when deciding to have a family. A mother has to sacrifice her body for the child even after the child is born. Mothers are shamed for breastfeeding in public and shamed for formula feeding.

We set our minds on how we want things to go, with our goals of breastfeeding until they're nine months old, or having a completely natural water birth, but our pregnancies and maternity experiences are controlled by the unpredictability of our bodies and the vulnerabilities of our humanness. For a person to put her mental health needs on pause for her baby is a sacrifice that I can only sympathize with. It was a beautiful letter, with perfect words, and a message that resonated with me deeply. The sacrifices we make for our babies, the love we give them, stems from generation to generation, and never ends.

In that moment, I heard the mailbox slam shut. The dogs went wild, and within milliseconds I heard Lola's bursting scream from the other room.

Now, that moment was gone—poor moms, poor nannies. God forbid you have a single second to yourself.

Those summer weeks went by slowly. Life moves slowly when you are alone with babies all day. They don't contribute to conversation, and the silence only makes the day go by like molasses. Toward the latter half of July, the nanny share was becoming a dysfunctional arrangement. After a few miscommunications between the mothers, and lack of awareness concerning the contagious nature of E. coli, one mother decided to resign from the nanny share.

The nanny share had enabled me to make what I needed to pay my rent, and allowed for the mothers to afford childcare, but without the mothers joining in together to pay me, I was simply unable to justify working for much less, and likewise, they were unable to afford me. As the summer dissipated and my job dissolved in only a matter of days, I became desperate. In a split second, I was forced to search for something new.

Déjà freaking vu.

By now, I was numb to it all. Like an out of body experience, unable to let myself feel, too jarred by yet another change. Learning my lesson for the third time now, that I should have had a contract with them, like with any other job, they would have at least given me two weeks' pay to hold me over. Instead, they got into their schools of choice, and the interim nanny, though extremely appreciated with kind words and thank you notes, was out there again to fend on her own with no contract and no rights.

I began asking myself the same questions that mothers ask themselves when they start to contemplate whether they can re-enter the workforce after staying home for a few years. I am certain my own mother wondered whether she would be able to keep up, whether she would even know what's going on anymore, or how to give herself any legitimacy in an interview when her previous work experience existed a few years ago. What is relevant? What were work-people talking about nowadays? Was I even relevant anymore? I felt stuck in nannying, like it had become my only skill. I had certainly mastered it, and I felt proud of supporting these families and taking good care of other humans—no one died, not one!

Even during the past summer, I had a handful of interviews, and a few nibbles at the line, but never a bite. I was concerned that I had lost my edge at only 27 years old.

Something was wrong with me.

Was I saying something wrong?

Had I lost everything I learned in undergraduate school?

Was I just going to be a caregiver forever?

That's the word that kills me— "just."

As if being a caregiver is easy, as if dealing with tantrums, and teething babies with E. Coli poisoning, and not taking the bottle is easy? Was watching two new parents sleep train their child and go to work sleep-deprived easy? It was not. Keeping a helpless little baby alive is a different strand of "hard work" that tests and triggers our most primal emotions. Often feeling impatient, frustrated, anxious, and paranoid, I could not treat this like any other job. People depended on me to be able to deal with it all, and it was beginning to feel like a heavy load to carry.

Along Came Baue

Kirsten knew me. She was 15 years my senior, and since she was also a teacher and ex-nonprofit slave, she knew exactly what stage of life I was in. Going from job to job, piecemealing gigs together, and falling into the nanny life, I was hoping to make a buck while soaking up time for reflection and contemplation. She knew that pulling the rug out from underneath me was a shitty thing to do, and by the grace of the universe, because Kirsten is such a hippie she probably doesn't believe in God anyway, she found me my fourth baby to watch that summer.

Mind you, it was only July. At this stage in my life I had spent more time one-on-one with infants than I might with my own child.

This merry-go-round of families had me thinking. Why would I even have a kid of my own? I'll just need to get a nanny to take care of it while I finally have the opportunity to pursue my career—assuming I will have one by my thirties.

This felt like wishful thinking.

Kirsten's neighbor had a five-month-old boy named Baue. They would joke and say he was baby Scarlet's boyfriend, also pale pink with rosacea cheeks, and a full head of dirty blonde straight hair. Scarlet equally as rosy-cheeked, they would procreate really nicely—way to put the cart before the horse.

Grace and Warren were typical, twenty-first century parents, always prefacing the fact that though they were banking on Scarlet and Baue becoming a future pair, they'd also be "totally fine" if Baue was gay. I found this refreshing and nice to know that parents now-a-days are way more open to whatever their child's pre-formed identity ends up becoming. Little signs of progress, I thought.

The parents were nervously anticipating a call from the daycare of their choice to give them the green light. "Any moment now they might call us," they said, "but the latest we expect to hear will be towards the middle of August."

That was vague and unpredictable, but cool, because I don't have a life to live and no plans for my future whatsoever. As long as your baby is cared for and you're able to go back to work, then screw it!

Being the nanny means your purpose and only purpose is to keep this family, baby, and home in line helping others achieve their goals, putting yours on hold, or getting more confused as you help them along while you're running on the treadmill of life. This is exactly why a stigma still exists that being a nanny isn't a real job. Even the family, who are factually the employers, are definitely not seeing their role as an employer; therefore, completely undermining the idea that nannies, in fact, are employees.

Baue's badass momma was a Public Defender and her husband was a sixth-grade mathematics teacher at a private school 30 minutes away. All had worked according to their plan. Yes, they planned this situation, and rightfully so, because the loans this woman had were likely astronomical, and we all know what teachers make in Colorado. She took her three-month government approved maternity leave and "coincidentally" the summer presented Dad with baby-duty until Baue was about five-and-a-half-months old which should certainly be long enough to get a baby into a preschool, right?

No. They were essentially in a state of panic. The clock was ticking and their baby had nowhere to go. These parents were in the same predicament as all the other ones. Forced to find childcare of their own, no family nearby to lend them a hand, and thus without the referral to hire me, they'd be completely out of luck.

Warren, the father, was starting school in a matter of days, and the mom had fiddled with her schedule enough to work four days a week, all of this to minimize the cost of paying a nanny any more than they needed to.

At this point, I had finally learned my lesson and created a contract. It was a really good one for that matter, one that ensured I'd be paid if the kids were sick and they needed to cancel last minute, one that required a signature so I would actually get paid my overtime, and one that included expectations and boundaries of what my work would, and would not, entail. Yes, I will do the dishes, the baby's laundry, and take out the trash when needed. No, I will not make appointments for you, wash your car, and walk your dog three times a day.

Did I mention I was becoming a pro at analyzing new parent behavior? There's got to be a future in that, right?

You see, new parents, especially first timers, are a bit unorganized and have a pretty unrealistic measurement of time. They forget how long it takes to take a shower, to run an errand,

and that you need two hands to make a sandwich. All tasks need eyes, ears, and hands to be readily available for a baby. This is often why nannies and sitters go unpaid for their overtime, and parents are simply too busy to notice. A contract of agreement between nannies and families can, and usually will, prevent this from happening if done correctly!

At this point, I had witnessed my own father in and out of town, flying airplanes and missing dance recitals. Danny's father was across the world from him in China. Gio's dad worked late. Ava and Martin's father was 1,000 miles away in Mississippi, and Callie's dad pretty much avoided her from what I could tell. He would rush home after he was off work, grab his gym bag, and whisper hello to me before ducking down to stay out of the baby's line of vision. He was trying to avoid any interaction that might lead to crying and, honestly, I don't blame him. She could really wail.

Yes, each Dad was "away" making money that undoubtedly allowed for their families to stay afloat and pay their nanny, but this doesn't negate the fact that their absence was still felt by both their child and partner.

Kirsten and Scarlet's life was the best example of what a life looks like without the help from a counterpart at all (especially a useless male one). Kirsten had carefully curated a collection of mostly female friends to support her before she decided to adopt Scarlet. With family far away, it was her friends and co-workers who would drop by with groceries, feed her chickens when she was out of town, and let her dogs out when she couldn't get home in time. Yes, she needed me and the nanny-share for a moment in time, but she was still 100 percent doing this mom thing on her own. She was set. No man—not even their sperm—was necessary for her to have her child and her life the way she wanted it. Talk about being an independent woman!

What I had observed in my first 27 years of life was that men had the ability to choose how much they wanted to be in their kids' lives or not, simply because the world, our society and culture, allowed them to. From my vantage point, all men seemed to be simply off the hook, and it was really starting to piss me off.

Then, along came Baue. Baue's family was the seventh family I would nanny for in three years, and I had noticed something remarkably different about them. It wasn't the contract. It wasn't their open-minded philosophy towards sexuality. It was his parents, and more specifically, his dad.

I had never witnessed a father invest so much time into his baby, or at least not to the level Warren did. In opposition to what the previous six families, seven, including my own upbringing, had proved to me, I was finally witnessing an anomaly.

Baue's dad, Warren, was the exception to the norm, and he was killin' the Dad game! Warren had been the stay-at-home dad for the past two months. He knew all the little details that typically only the mom knows, such as what pacifier Baue liked the most, which song calmed him down, and what his breathing sounded like when he was finally asleep. Warren trained me on how to keep the breast milk from going bad, when feedings should take place, and how to finagle the stroller safely out of the backyard gate. He gave me the insider knowledge of where the best walking-distance coffee shops were and where the closest park was with a baby swing.

I was impressed, to say the least, and this experience gave me hope that men were becoming better fathers and better partners, hope that things were changing, that our world, including women—the wives and mothers—were beginning to expect more of the men in their lives, require more of their time, and actually require their presence.

Baue's family was a sign, a sign that my generation was doing something right, a sign that maybe waiting until we are 30 to 35 years old to get married and settle down has more to do with truly being ready for commitment rather than the assumption that we are avoiding it.

We want to be ready. We want to be intentional. Baue's family was so intentional about everything, and the only thing that hadn't worked completely according to plan was needing a nanny.

It was the childcare system, or lack thereof, that was the culprit here. How is it that the last four families, back to back, needed me to help them so suddenly? I recognized this pattern as something larger, a symptom of a political and institutional issue that was having real negative effects on growing families' finances, careers, marriages, and wellbeing.

"It's like we should have put our baby on this waitlist before they were even conceived," one mom exclaimed. "How were we supposed to know that Denver has no affordable options for day care? Doesn't everybody need daycare nowadays?"

"I'm basically going to work to pay for childcare. It's a scam, I swear. I should just stay at home."

One family shared their issue: "We're too poor to afford a nanny long term, and too rich to qualify for the free daycare at the public schools, so we have to wait it out at our local daycare that is trying to accommodate a waitlist that's over 85 families long. It's a lose-lose."

Their urgent need for emergency childcare was beyond their control, as they had seemingly done everything right. A few weeks after the babies were born, and while some were still in utero. These parents were researching their nearby daycares and pre-schools, analyzing their budgets, fidgeting with their calendars, planning with their employers, and banking on their three months of maternity leave to be enough time to find childcare.

Three months should have given them plenty of time, right?

Wrong.

Simply put, the local daycares didn't have enough spots to accommodate the number of babies needing care.

This was a city-wide problem for Denver, and what also appeared to be a nationwide issue. Early Head Start programs were available for those living under the poverty line, but for households making more than $43,000 a year, they had to fend for themselves.

As a middle-class millennial myself, I am scared for what might happen when I have children. How will I possibly afford it? I was honestly worried.

Millennials are people born between 1981 through 1996, and currently they are approximately 23 to 38 years old and now make up more than 35 percent of the working population. Reported in 2018 by PEW Research center, "Some 1.2 million millennial women gave birth for the first time in 2016. National Center for Health Statistics data raised the total number of U.S. women in this generation who have become mothers to more than 17 million." (NCHS, 2019)

With nowhere to take their children, one mother said, "Either you choose to stay at home or you pay an arm and a leg to send them to daycare. Either way, you're paying some kind of price just to keep them alive."

There is no secret to the madness. It's a systemic problem that undermines working families and their ability to financially get ahead, or save for their kids to go to college or pay their mortgages. In addition, millennials are also a generation that has experienced much of their professional careers after the 2009 economic crisis, experiencing higher unemployment than their parents' generation, and now they are reaching the years of marriage and family planning, all while looking at the next 20 to 30 years of paying off student debt.

Callie's family, Scarlet's family, Lola's Family, and Baue's family have all been victims of this issue in their own right, yet I, as their nanny was the beneficiary of such a system. The demand for childcare is there, and a percentage of millennial women, the ones who are predominantly younger and childless, have seized the opportunity to supply this demand by becoming nannies. In fact, they have become some of the most experienced and educated nannies and caregivers seen to date.

With supply and demand fueling our capitalistic economy, our country has made childcare a commodity. For quantity, you will get quality. Forced to buy childcare resources, American families are all going to market for the best we can get without scraping the barrel. This is not an equal system, and it is in fact a major contributor to the cycle of poverty for low-income women with children who are trying to become self-sufficient.

All these truths have become so painstakingly clear to me at this point. When perceiving a social phenomenon, and witnessing repeated patterns of human behavior, one has to wonder why our world is the way it is and what it would take for things to change.

Even if the time I spent caring for Baue was solely for my benefit, I am so grateful they needed me, because I needed them. I needed their example of what a reciprocal partnership looks like, and a positive, present, and plugged-in example of fatherhood.

Warren, like every mother I had worked for at this same stage in her life, seemed ready for change. Cooped up all day without any interaction from other adults is hard. He was ready to get back to school and leave the nest. I will never know if he cried in his car on his way back to work, or if he felt the biological pull that mothers feel when they leave their children, but I can imagine he had the same feeling when I left Danny back in California, like a limb from his body was missing, and it would take a little while for the brain to recalibrate and process the physical loss.

I respected this Dad for the time he spent with his son. Why is it that I had respect for him, but never once thought about the respect I had for the mothers who had been at home? I know, it's a double standard.

He had a bond with his baby that most men, other than those in countries with paternity leave, do not have the luxury of getting. He generally trusted me, as I had more experience with infants than he and his wife combined, and the only worry he really had was making sure the baby didn't lick the walls.

Yes, lick the walls.

Lead paint had been used to paint most homes in Denver before the 1970s and, thus, Warren had put up what looked like a mini horse's corral to confine Baue to the dining room area. This, indeed, prevented him from being in licking distance of the walls—good dad move, I must say.

During the month I spent time with Baue, I was trying to finish an online course about organizational leadership. Nothing feels more awkward than writing a discussion post referencing my former professional life like it was currently happening. In reality, I was cleaning up baby vomit and folding a stranger's maternity clothes that had to be washed constantly because she only seemed to have a total of five shirts on rotation. Minimalism is great until you want to skip laundry day.

Amidst day trips to the park with Baue and anticipating my next steps, I was offered a proposition I could not refuse. An opportunity I had been waiting for unexpectedly revealed itself to me as if orchestrated by God. A former professor had contacted me. She was my mentor in college, a real social-justice community organizer, a blonde, white lady who was hell-bent on making things right for underserved communities. She was a woman I had admired for being smart as hell and using her privilege and power for good. What I loved most, is that I could confidently say she was making a real change in the world—well, at least in Lafayette, Colorado.

She was reviving a small nonprofit in East Boulder County, where the public school district had forgotten about a few of their lower-performing schools where the graduation rate was lower than the rest, and not surprisingly, they happened to have some of the highest numbers of Spanish-speaking, first-generation students of color. I hate how predictable this stuff is. She needed me to join her as she rebranded and revived the organization to better serve the young people in East Boulder County.

This part of Boulder County housed a higher number of low-income residents and experienced a notably higher rate of substance abuse in comparison to the rest of the area. Her theory, which can ring true for many small towns across America, is that youth agencies, devoted to serving young people in all areas of life—both academic and developmental—provide programs and efforts that help to intervene and prevent things from getting worse. This is her life's work, alongside working to renew democracy in U.S. public education by performing direct service to her community. It is very impressive, and very depleting, selfless, and most of all, difficult to do this work.

During the following year, I worked alongside her as we built programs for young people to gain mentors, access opportunities to further themselves, and create service projects that empowered their communities. Baue's number was called at the local preschool, and I transitioned from interim nanny to Program Director of the Empowerment Center of East County.

In my eyes, this was my big break. This was the job I'd been waiting for and manifesting since I started nannying almost three years ago. This was the opportunity that not only would allow me to feel legitimatized as a person, but it would allow me to implement my course work appropriately.

Leaving a baby never felt so good, not that Baue was easy to leave. He was super cute and cuddly, but I had my baby-fix. I couldn't help but feel that it would be the last and final time that I would spend with a child that wasn't my own. I was more than okay with that and itching to move forward.

CHAPTER SIXTEEN

Pieces of Peace

As we negotiated the terms of the contract for my "real" job, I agreed to make less than I had been nannying. This was the Catch 22.

Though opportunity had presented itself, and I would in fact be able to utilize my education and reference my actual professional life in my discussion boards, I still needed to babysit to make some side cash. I take that back. It was just regular cash I needed to make, like the kind that would pay my cell phone bill and car insurance, like necessary cash for survival.

Most millennials drive for a ride share company or pour beer on the weekends. I watch people's kids.

Babysitting for me had become one of the cogs in what we are now calling "the gig economy." I continued to occasionally watch Callie, Scarlet, Lola, and Baue, and as these cute little babies grew up, so did I. My social life grew. My relationship with Jay had flourished, and my first shot at entrepreneurship was under way.

I finished my online degree, and by my 28th birthday in the spring of 2017, I had finally earned my master's degree. This felt amazing.

Though this degree would come in handy one day, I still knew in the back of my head that a master's degree in teaching and learning would never make enough to be considered "successful" in my eyes. Success equals wealthy, but teaching does not make one wealthy. The comparison of how far I'd come, to what was reflected in my bank account, didn't make sense to me. I felt like I'd made it to the top of my own figurative mountain, but now that I was at the top, all I could see were the other mountains I still needed to climb.

Leadership Theorist, Author, and Ted-Talker Simon Sinek spoke about millennials having an abstract concept of what it means to "make an impact." He explained that the impact they speak of is essentially this illusion of a summit that millennials have been conditioned to believe they can conquest without fail. He explained that what they don't see is the mountain leading up to the summit, and the long, arduous journey that requires time, patience, and perspective to accomplish.

I also know that I get this yearning from my father who was always haunted by his own success. With every accomplishment, every raise, every bonus came the self-inflicted pressure that he had to keep moving to the next big thing. He rarely gave himself time to enjoy the fruits of his labor and rather kept himself in a constant purgatory, feeling like nothing will ever amount to enough. We felt this pressure as his family and absorbed this mentality in our own ways. My younger sister had watched me pursue a degree that seemed to get me nowhere, so she earned a degree in the medical field which would "set her up for life" as my Dad would put it.

Money did this to me. Money made me second guess my personal definition of success. Money made me beat myself up rather than celebrate my accomplishments. The irony of our world had hit me straight in the face. The most necessary jobs, that primarily women were performing, are grossly underpaid and certainly don't get the praise and attention they deserve.

Why did I even choose to study teaching? It was the only topic I really knew and felt I could master, literally. Twenty-five percent of my job with the nonprofit was teaching, instruction, and designing lessons, but the other 75 percent was community organizing, and that was what I loved the most.

After exploring the cost of a teaching licensure in the state of Colorado, which was about $4,000, and imagining my fate teaching for a school, I knew that I couldn't, or merely didn't want to, sign up for it. I didn't want to sign up to get paid pennies, to be treated like scum by eighth graders, and then go home to grade their papers until 8 p.m. every night. I saw my teacher friends and what they were doing. I so admired them for their hard work, their grit, and their perseverance, but I'm not sure I'd have the endurance to get to Thanksgiving break without having a nervous breakdown from the pressure.

I feel bitter and resentful when I face these truths about myself, combined with learning more about the glass ceiling women are trying to break through in so many professions. I couldn't help but feel at a loss.

"Being a woman sucks!" I burst into my therapist's office. This was the last session we would have in a long time and I could feel the swelling of my throat as I became completely unhinged in her office. "I just feel like no matter what profession or direction I go I am going to end up doing peoples' dishes and helping people get to their next step in their career while I just stay stagnant and left behind in the dust."

"I know you are really struggling with gender roles right now, and combined with your family history and your father's struggle with alcohol, you have every right to feel that way," my therapist said. She was great at validating my feelings, but this time she called me out. "But you're really good at being a woman."

I asked, "What do you mean by that?" At this point I was completely appalled by her statement.

She explained: "You're giving and kind. You listen and do things for other people. You are a caring and motherly person whether you think you'll ever have a child or not. This is your role in people's lives around you."

I thought that my therapist was a little off that day. It's like she was telling me this as a friend. "You are a caregiver for those around you, like, beyond being a Nanny. If that's not the most extensive set of womanly characteristics, I don't know what is."

She paused for a moment, and I was silent. "You are a woman, and that's why the world needs you to keep being exactly what you are."

I couldn't help but feel overwhelmed by her words. She was right, that my skill set, which many other women also possess, is best suited in roles that position me to assist others, but I want to be more than that. I want people to also see my skill set as those that a leader, a boss, a manager, or someone in charge possesses.

I marched in the Women's March in downtown Denver that year. I watched Hillary Clinton lose to a sexist pig of a man and I vowed to myself that I would do my part in making positive social change for women, especially those who are historically disenfranchised. Even though my sister's career in the medical field would guarantee that her job search would never look like mine, a career in caretaking comes with sacrifice, physical sacrifice, psychological sacrifice, and also financial sacrifice.

I felt empowered to make moves that year, literally and metaphorically. Jay and I had mended what had been broken and were anticipating a move to Austin, Texas. Moving, as we've learned, made me reflect. It forced me to leave things behind and drive straight into the unknown. Jay and I packed our things and moved 917.5 miles together. This move was a metaphor for leaving the struggle of my past behind in Colorado and create a new path for myself with my soon-to-be life partner.

I would no longer have to watch other peoples' kids, drive in the snow, or have to keep working in my underpaying nonprofit job. I now had the opportunity to start over and use my powers for good.

My special power, I had learned, is caring for others. It is listening and counseling, helping and empowering other women to problem-solve and keep going. Though I do this for my friends, for my co-workers, and even strangers I meet, I am still looking for how this ability will impact my life's story.

I decided to start here by writing this book, and allowing my stories to thank the women in my life and those who came before me. Diving deep into memories of Teen allowed me to see her story through a historical lens which in turn, allowed me to see my own story with a different perspective. I learned how to be objective, to face history, and to recognize that all women are contributing to history, even if they are "just a nanny."

At 29 years old, I'm still trying to figuring out what I want to do with my life and have found myself in various office and administrative roles. I quit the highest paying job I had ever had to try out my shot at nonprofit consulting and contract work. I reactivated my Care.com account a few times, finding a few moms to help out every now and then, and then wrote the majority of this book that year.

At 29 and half years old, I worked at a school, starting as a substitute and ending up as the receptionist. I spent half a year helping an all-female staff turn around a first-year charter school. The school went from a community rating of a 'D' to an 'A' in just six months. I was paid $13.00 per hour and never got promoted. I got married that fall and recruited to fill a receptionist role for one of the world's largest social media companies.

The adventure continues, and at 31 years old, in 2020, not much has changed. I'm still not wealthy and still wondering if I will ever go back to teaching one day.

In every role I have had, every family, every school, every short-term project, the constant is me. I am the help they needed to get to their next stop in life. Doing this work has also helped me in a multitude of ways. What I have learned through my experiences is that every job matters, whether you find yourself nannying, busing tables, answering phones at a call center, cleaning an elementary school, or all the other predominantly female, service-based roles we are performing. The world would not turn without us.

As an ode to my twenties, I wrote this book to share the complexity that is a millennial woman's journey. With so many factors at play, I hope that my story can help other women know the value of their work no matter the pay or the position. As I am not nearly finished with my journey, I have come to find pieces of my life to come to peace with, laying them to rest and allowing the space to be filled with love, acceptance, and revived hope in my role on earth. My wish is that you will find pieces of peace in your past as well. Thank you for reading my story. I send you all the best in living out your life's purpose.

We Are Generation Nanny

A few companies have capitalized on the nanny sector, creating online platforms that expedite the searching, vetting, and hiring process it takes to find a nanny. Care.com made $53.3 million in the third quarter of 2019, increasing their revenue by eight percent from the previous year. Sitter City and Urban Sitter are also massive online platforms helping to match families with nearby sitters. All of these companies are successful due to the demand for easy, free, safe, and fast ways to find childcare. This is the childcare market catering to millennial parents, their needs and preferences, by allowing them to set filters and categories to find their perfect nanny. As a result, women who are primarily young, educated, and have access to technology benefit from this directly.

My experience as a nanny is a prime example of this systematic privilege, which is why my first call to action is for families to utilize local nanny agencies that work with the National Domestic Workers Alliance (NDWA) to protect and empower some of the most vulnerable caretakers, house cleaners, nannies, and more from exploitation and harassment.

The existence of NDWA alone helps to legitimize the nanny or caregiver, as someone who is actively performing a job. Jobs require pay, parameters, expectations, limits, and therefore, caregivers are defined as people who are not merely existing in the shadows of our homes, but are employees who have rights and should be protected by laws. Care.com provides resources for nannies and families on taxes, healthcare, mileage reimbursement forms, and even makes an effort to update the living wage page on their website.

Even with all of these resources provided, nannies, housekeepers, and caregivers are still some of the most vulnerable workers, who experience lost wages and limited access to healthcare, retirement, paid time off, and unlike other jobs, they do not have a human resources department to run to when they experience workplace harassment, abuse, or mistreatment. According to NDWA, 2.5 million nannies, housecleaners, and care workers go to work every day, and the majority of these workers are predominantly women, immigrants, and women of color. NDWA was founded in 2007 and works for the respect, recognition, and inclusion in labor protections for domestic workers.

What happens now?

In 2020, though the internet has changed how we find help, the way we view domestic workers and the work they do has not changed much. We now have the opportunity to change this.

It's time to make real change. We are all Generation Nanny. Families, mothers, nannies, sitters, young women and seasoned veteran caregivers. Progress is being made, and Generation Nanny is a community that will move the needle forward through storytelling, organizing, and action.

Call to Action

A call to action for nannies:

- Make a contract, even if it's a temporary arrangement or an occasional babysitting gig. Protect yourself and treat it like a real job. Nannies can find a template to make your own agreement for employment on GenerationNanny.com

- Ask for what you want: hourly wage, benefits, PTO, sick time, gas and mileage, spending money, stipend for extra expenses. The worst employers can do is say no.

- Join the National Domestic Workers Alliance at domesticworkers.org/. Know your rights and stand up for what you deserve.

A call to action for families:

- Make a contract as any employer would.

- Provide training for your nanny, and don't expect them to read your mind.

- Be honest about having nanny-cam/video cameras in your home.

- Pay your nanny the going rate of your city and state or more!

- When hiring a nanny, consider nannies of color and those of immigrant status to counter some of the displacement that is happening in the Nanny industry today.

- Join the National Domestic Workers Alliance, and familiarize yourself with the Bill of Rights.

About The Author

Audrey Brazeel calls herself a Creative Connector, which she defines as being a creative who uses their expertise and specialized skill set in writing and design to build community around them. She loves working with nonprofits, coordinating community projects, and empowering women to be their best selves.

The release of this book stands as a major personal accomplishment, and writing it has given her the purpose she is in fact searching for throughout her book. Audrey has always been a floater, jumping from job to job and place to place. As she bounces from one thing to the next, she considers every experience as research. Meeting people is her way of collecting data, and writing is her outlet to share her findings. She has a Bachelor of Arts degree in Anthropology and Ethnic Studies from University of Colorado Boulder and earned a Master of Science degree in Teaching and Learning, with a specialization in Organizational Leadership and Change Management from Colorado State University, Global Campus.

As Audrey begins her 30s, she hopes publishing her work will help her to put her 20s to rest and allow her to embrace the next decade. She hopes her book will help other 20-somethings embrace the mundane service jobs that are often done to pass the time as purposeful moments meant to teach and lead us closer to our destinations.

Connect GenerationNanny.com | @GenerationNanny

Made in the USA
Monee, IL
14 July 2020

36556236R00104